ON THE MOTHER OF GOD

ST VLADIMIR'S SEMINARY PRESS
Popular Patristics Series
Number 19

The Popular Patristics Series published by St Vladimir's Seminary Press provides readable and accurate translations of a wide range of early Christian literature to a wide audience—students of Christian history to lay Christians reading for spiritual benefit. Recognized scholars in their fields provide short but comprehensive and clear introductions to the material. The texts include classics of Christian literature, thematic volumes, collections of homilies, letters on spiritual counsel, and poetical works from a variety of geographical contexts and historical backgrounds. The mission of the series is to mine the riches of the early Church and to make these treasures available to all.

Series Editor
BOGDAN BUCUR

Associate Editor
IGNATIUS GREEN

* * *

Series Editor
1999–2020
JOHN BEHR

On the
Mother of God

JACOB OF SERUG

Translation by
MARY HANSBURY

Introduction by
SEBASTIAN BROCK

ST VLADIMIR'S SEMINARY PRESS

YONKERS, NEW YORK

Library of Congress Cataloging-in-Publication Data

Jacob, of Serug, 451–521
  [Marian homilies. Homily 1–3. English]
  On the Mother of God / Jacob of Serug; translation by Mary Hansbury, introduction by Sebastian Brock.
    p. cm.
  Includes bibliographical references.
    ISBN 0–88141–184–1 (alk. paper)
    1. Mary, Blessed Virgin, Saint—Sermons 2. Sermons, Syriac—Translations into English. 3. Mary, Blessed Virgin, Saint—Poetry. 4. Christian poetry, Syriac—Translations into English. I. Hansbury, Mary. II. Jacob, of Serug, 451–521. Marian homilies. Homily 5. English. III. Title
    BT608.J3313 1998
    232.91—dc21

Copyright © 1998 by
St Vladimir's Seminary Press
575 Scarsdale Road, Yonkers, NY 10707
1–800–204–2665
www.svspress.com

ISBN 978-0-88141-184-3 (paper)
ISBN 978-0-88141-751-7 (electronic)

Printed in the United States of America

Table of Contents

Translator's Note

The translation is made from Fr Paul Bedjan's edition of the Syriac text in *S. Martyrii, qui et Sahdona quae supersunt omnia* (Paris/Leipzig: Otto Harrassowitz, 1902). The homilies that I have translated are: Homily 1, B.614–B.639; Homily 2, B.639–B.661; Homily 3, B.661–B.685; and Homily 5, B.709–B.719. The numbers of the corresponding pages in Bedjan are printed throughout this volume.

An Italian translation of these and other homilies of Jacob may be found in Costantino Vona, *Omelie mariologiche di S. Giacomo di Sarug* (Rome: Lateran University Press, 1953).

The anonymous Syriac Life of Jacob of Serug included here is preserved in Ms Vat Syr 37, 16r. and was published by J. S. Assemani, *Bibliotheca Orientalis* 1 (Rome: Society for the Propagation of the Faith, 1719), 286–289.

Gratitude is due to the faculty and staff of St Vladimir's Seminary for their continued support of Syriac studies. Also, I offer this book to the memory of Fr Giuseppi Dossetti, whose love of the Mother of God and of Scripture, and his conviction of the importance of the Syriac tradition for the life of the Church, have sustained me in this translation.

A final word, one of gratitude, to Fr John Meyendorff, who continues to inspire and encourage from Abraham's bosom.

Mary Hansbury
Feast of the Annunciation, 1998

Bibliographical Note

Ephrem's poems are quoted from the recent edition (with German translation) by Dom E. Beck, in the Louvain Corpus of oriental Christian writers, while Jacob of Serug's Marian homilies are quoted from Paul Bedjan's edition, at the end of his *S. Martyrii qui et Sahdona quae supersunt omnia* (1902; Italian translation by Costantino Vona, Rome: Lateran University Press, 1953).

For some further aspects of Marian typology reference may be made to Robert Murray, S.J., "Mary, the Second Eve in the Early Syriac Fathers," in *Eastern Churches Review* 3 (Holywell Press, 1971), 372–84; and "The lance which re-opened Paradise, a mysterious reading in the early Syriac Fathers," in *Orientalia Christiana Periodica* 39 (Rome: Pontificium Institutum Orientalium Studiorum, 1973), 224–34, 491. English translations of some relevant hymns of Ephrem will be found in the following: Robert Murray, "A Hymn of St. Ephrem to Christ on the Incarnation, the Holy Spirit, and the Sacraments," *Eastern Churches Review* 3 (Holywell Press, 1970): 142–50; *Symbols of Church and Kingdom* (Cambridge, 1975); Sebastian P. Brock, *The Bride of Light: Hymns on Mary from the Syriac Churches* (Kottayam, India: St Ephrem Ecumenical Research Institute [SEERI], 1994); "St. Ephrem on Christ as Light in Mary and in the Jordan," *Eastern Churches Review* 7 (Holywell Press, 1976): 137–44; *The Harp of the Spirit: Eighteen Poems of St. Ephrem* (Studies Supplementary to *Sobornost* 4, 2nd ed., London: Fellowship of St. Alban and St. Sergius, 1983); and *The Luminous Eye: The Spiritual World Vision of St. Ephrem* (2nd ed., Kalamazoo, MI: Cistercian Publications, 1992).

Introduction

Since Syriac literature will be somewhat *terra incognita* to many, it may be helpful to begin by charting out very briefly something of the territory. Syriac is a dialect of Aramaic, the language spoken by Jesus; it is related to Hebrew and Arabic, and it became the literary language of Christians living in the most easterly part of the Roman Empire, as well as those living further east still, in the Persian or Sassanid Empire (roughly modern Iraq and Iran). Thus, from the first, it became the liturgical and literary language for the churches in this area, and it still survives today in its role as a liturgical language in the Maronite Church in Lebanon, and in the Syrian Orthodox Church and the Church of the East (or to use the sobriquets for the latter two that are more familiar in the West, the Jacobite or Monophysite, and the Nestorian Churches), together with their Uniate counterparts.

Because it was transmitted in ecclesiastical circles, almost all Syriac literature that survives is Christian, and the earliest literary texts go back perhaps to the second century AD, but it is not until the fourth century that the sources become at all extensive. The golden age of Syriac literature may be said to extend from the fourth to the sixth century; at any rate this is the period of the best and most creative examples of that literary genre in which Syriac writers excelled—namely, liturgical poetry. This does not mean to say that the literature came to an end with the Arab conquests in the seventh century—in fact a great deal has continued to be written in Syriac right up to the present day.

Here I shall make use only of texts from the golden age of Syriac literature, employing in particular the writings of two of the greatest of all Syriac poets, St Ephrem who died in 373, and Jacob of Serug, a Syrian Orthodox writer who flourished around the turn of the fifth/

sixth century. Most of the themes I shall deal with could equally well be illustrated from the liturgical texts of both the Syrian Orthodox and the East Syrian (Nestorian and Chaldean) traditions, which in fact often draw extensively on Ephrem and Jacob; and here attention may be drawn to what at first may seem a surprising fact: Nestorius is well known to all as having rejected the title of *Theotokos*, "bearer of God," for Mary, and in view of this one might have expected the East Syrian liturgical texts to be less concerned than their Syrian Orthodox counterparts with the role of Mary, but this is in fact far from the case: the general tone of both traditions is very similar. In actual fact, the Christological differences that separate the Syrian Orthodox, Greek Orthodox (Chalcedonian) Churches and the Church of the East do not appear to have had much effect on their attitudes to Mary, at least outside technical theological discussions. Thus, those who are familiar with the Byzantine tradition will find much of what Syriac writers say on the subject of Mary not unfamiliar.

My choice of poetic, rather than prose, texts is deliberate. There is a large corpus of pseudepigraphical literature about Mary in prose in Syriac, as well as a small amount of specifically theological writing, but it is the poetic texts that provide by far the most sympathetic treatment, and their approach—essentially suggestive, avoiding cut and dried dogmatic statements—is one that seems to have a real validity.

There remains one final introductory point: the language that Syriac writers use of Mary is very largely biblical, or inspired by the Bible. The Syriac-speaking churches possess their own Bible, of very great antiquity, the standard text being known as the Peshitta, the Old Testament translated directly from the Hebrew, the New from the Greek. This means that there are a number of differences between the Syriac, Greek, and Latin Bibles, and these of course, to a certain extent, have influenced the interpretation of individual passages. For the New Testament there was actually another, earlier, translation available, but of this only the Gospels survive; this, rather than the Peshitta New Testament, was the text known to Ephrem, along with a second-century harmony of the four Gospels, known as the *Diatessaron*. This earliest New Testament translation was considerably freer than the Peshitta, and the *Diatessaron* in particular introduced into the Gospel text certain apocryphal elements, such as the bright light accompanying the Baptism of Christ in the Jordan. Finally, an important fact to remember is that the Apocalypse did not form part of the original Syriac New Testament canon, and it was not translated into Syriac until the early sixth century.

To begin, I take a rather surprising text—a Syriac Orthodox calendar copied in North Iraq in 1689. Commenting on the feasts of March, the compiler states: "As for the Feast of the Annunciation, the Church celebrates it on whichever day of the week the twenty-fifth falls: even if it falls on Good Friday, we still celebrate the Liturgy, since the Annunciation is the beginning and source of all other feasts." This text excellently exemplifies the emphasis one finds, throughout Syriac literature, that the Annunciation, and Mary's role there, is the crucial starting point for the events of the Incarnation: in other words, the view is taken that, without Mary, the Incarnation would not have taken place.

The vital role played by Mary at the Annunciation is a theme developed at some length by Jacob of Serug in a famous series of metrical homilies on the Virgin. In the first place Mary is chosen as being worthy of Gabriel's visitation because she is the most perfect mortal ever to have lived:

> Because God saw her, and how pure and clear her soul,
> He wished to dwell in her who had been purified from every
>   wickedness,
> for no woman had ever appeared like her. (B. 622)

And a little further on Jacob bluntly states:

> Had any other woman pleased Him more than Mary,
> He would have chosen her instead.

Mary is, however, by no means a tool of divine providence in Jacob's eyes; in a dramatic dialogue between her and Gabriel, Mary cross-questions the angel for she recalls how Eve had fallen through unquestioningly accepting the serpent's suggestion. Jacob comments:

> Through Eve's silence came defeat and disrepute,
> through Mary's words, Life, Light, and victory. (B. 631)

Everything depends on Mary's answer to the angel. Jacob firmly rejects the view, apparently current, that the Word entered Mary's womb *before* the angel had spoken, thus implying that her answer was a foregone conclusion; rather, in his view,

> The moment she replied in the affirmative,
> she conceived (lit. received the Fruit) in her womb. (B. 739)

Before leaving the Annunciation, three rather individual features of Syriac tradition in connection with it should be mentioned. First, the Logos, or Word, is regarded as having entered Mary quite literally through her ear:

> Through her ear the Word entered and dwelt secretly in the womb. (Attributed to Ephrem, *H. Mary* 11.6)

Ephrem's words here represent a commonplace among Syriac writers. As we shall see, this—to us somewhat bizarre—idea was popular for typological reasons, Mary's obedience being contrasted with Eve's disobedience.

The second feature is an exegesis of Luke 1.35, "the Holy Spirit shall come upon you, and the Power of the Most High shall overshadow you," which is developed notably by Jacob of Serug, but which is by no means confined to him. On a number of occasions Jacob is careful to differentiate between the "Spirit" and the "Power," the "Spirit" being the Holy Spirit who first sanctifies Mary's womb, and the "Power" being the Word, who then enters and dwells there. The basic reason for this exegesis is evidently a grammatical consideration: in Syriac *ruha,* "spirit," is feminine and in early Syriac literature the Holy Spirit, *ruha d-qudsha,* is mostly construed grammatically as a feminine, although later on, under Greek influence, it was treated as a masculine (Syriac having no neuter). The word for "Power" on the other hand is masculine (whereas *dynamis* of the Greek is feminine). One might have thought that this grammatical feature, the spirit being feminine, would have played an important role in the way the Syriac-speaking church thought of the Holy Spirit, but with a few notable exceptions, among which the exegesis of Luke 1.35 is one, this has apparently not been the case—at least in the texts that survive.

The third feature is of rather a different order and concerns the calendar. In the East Syrian tradition, the period known as Advent in the West is called the "Annunciation," thus laying stress once more on the intimate relationship between Mary's initial acceptance and the consequence of the Incarnation and the Nativity.

I shall in fact pass very quickly over the theme of the Nativity, since I wish to dwell at rather more length on the subject of Mary and the Old Testament. Syriac writers regularly stress Mary's perpetual virginity but regard it as a mystery that should not be pried into. According to Jacob of Serug, some people posed the dilemma: "If the Incarnation is a reality, then virginity *in partu* is impossible; but if Mary remained a virgin *in partu,* then the Incarnation was not real." Jacob rejects this as a false dilemma, since it takes no account of the "miracle" of the Incarnation itself—such a miraculous event takes place in a miraculous way, breaking the physiological laws of nature. This sort of attitude is very much in line with that of the Greek Fathers, and, as we shall shortly see, it was given a typological basis.

Let us now turn to the subject of Mary and the Old Testament. Early Syriac exegesis of the Bible was essentially typological—that is to say, connections between persons, objects, and events were sought out and brought together, either as complementing or as contrasting each other. This typological exegesis can take on two main forms: on the one hand, it can be purely historical, confined to the framework of the biblical revelation: Paul's Adam-Christ typology belongs to this category, and we shall shortly be concerned in particular with the Eve-Mary typology, first found in Justin Martyr, in the second century. On the other hand, the typological relationships can also be between this world and the heavenly world, and this variety can best be described as symbolic typology. Very often both kinds of typology, historical and symbolic, are used simultaneously, and frequently in a very elaborate way.

To Ephrem's fertile mind these types or symbols (in Syriac they are usually called "mysteries") are to be found everywhere, and on one occasion he self-mockingly complains:

> This Jesus has made so many symbols that I have fallen into the sea of them.

Ephrem's highly allusive poetry, shifting almost relentlessly from one set of symbols to another, makes considerable demands on the reader who, above all, if he is to appreciate Ephrem to the full, must know his Bible as well as Ephrem did. Much of this typological exegesis will appear to modern readers as forced, or it may even be described as "wrong," but I think it is misleading to speak of this kind of exegesis in absolute terms of "correct" and "incorrect." The very fact that quite often one finds side by side two pieces of typological exegesis that are logically incompatible when taken together seems to be an indication that what is being offered was never meant to be "the correct exegesis," such as modern biblical scholarship likes to impose, but possible models that are held up and whose purpose is to make meaningful, and give insight into, some aspects of a mystery that cannot be fully explained.

One might perhaps view Ephrem and his fellow poet-exegetes as offering to their readers a garden full of every kind of flower; their readers are the bees, which, as they go around collecting honey, enjoy the fragrance of all the flowers as a whole, but each individual bee will alight only on those particular flowers that take its fancy.

This method of exegesis is in fact essentially meant as an aid to devotional contemplation, and as such, it seems to me to be eminently successful. That it is definitely mythopoeic in character should not be considered as detracting from its value, for mythology, in the proper sense of the word, is precisely what mankind has always used to help explain what is beyond the bounds of full human comprehension: it simply provides possible analogies and models—precisely what the Syriac poets are doing.

Furthermore, what these poets are offering is not only spiritual delights, but also aesthetic ones, for typological exegesis has also been developed into something of an art-form, where the external symmetry of the—often intricate—typological pattern is also meant to please, quite apart from its inner spiritual content.

Syriac writers saw an abundance of types and symbols of Mary when they read their Bibles, and in passing it is worth noting that the vast majority of these types (e.g., "ark," "temple," "cruse," "chariot,") are objects that *contain* something holy—in other words they are essentially Christocentric in character. Here I shall confine myself to one particular area that is of basic importance: the Eve-Mary typology.

At the outset it will be helpful to note various distinctions in the way this parallelism is applied. Paul's First Adam-Second Adam typology would demand as a logical extension the equation of Mary, not with Eve, but with the earth from which the First Adam sprang. This pattern is indeed found in Syriac writers. As Ephrem puts it:

> The virgin earth of old gave birth to the Adam who is lord of the earth,
> but today another Virgin has given birth to the Adam who is Lord of heaven. *(H. Nativ.* 1.16)

Here the aspect emphasized is the mother-child relationship, given in simple, contrasted form. Ephrem actually provides in this poem a more subtle and intricate piece of typology, for he combines this with the parallelism between Adam, the begetter of Eve, and Mary, the bearer of Christ; once again the interest is in the genetic relationship, and in particular in its miraculous nature:

> Adam brought forth travail upon the woman who sprang from him, but today she (Mary), who bore him a Savior, has redeemed that travail. A man (Adam) who himself knew no birth, bore Eve the mother: how much more should Eve's daughter (Mary) be believed to have given birth without the aid of a man! (*H. Nativ.* 1.14–15)

The same idea is found in Jacob:

> As our father (Adam) begot our mother without intercourse, so did Mary give birth, just as Adam did before he had sinned. The Holy Spirit blew on Adam's face, and he gave birth to Eve: this Spirit did Mary too receive, and she gave birth to a Son. Adam gave birth to the "mother of all living things" without intercourse, thus depicting the birth of our Lord, who is the fountain of all life. (B. 634)

Here the pattern Adam:Eve—Mary:Christ is a twofold one, for Ephrem and Jacob quite certainly see this as a chiastic arrangement as well: Mary corresponds to Adam in her miraculous childbearing, but at the same time she also corresponds to Eve; and Christ to Adam, following the customary typology.

The prime concern of the long-established Eve-Mary typology, to which we now turn, is of course the contrast between fall and restoration, and not relationships, as in the previous examples. There appear to be two rather different ways of looking at this contrast between Eve and Mary. On the one hand, one can take a cyclical view of salvation history and regard Mary as reversing what Eve brought about, in which case Mary starts off, as it were, in the position into which Eve had reduced the human race, but through the Incarnation Mary is able to bring mankind back into Paradise, the pre-fall state. I shall call this the "dynamic" view. On the other hand, one can regard Mary's position as having been *throughout* her life that of Eve *before* the fall. This I shall call the "static" view. Now the dynamic view is quite certainly the earlier, and as far as I can see, the normal view of the Fathers, of whatever language; it is certainly the view of Ephrem and Jacob, the two Syriac poets who have the most to say on the subject of Mary.

Since, however, most writers were interested in describing Mary only in the light of the Incarnation, they naturally refer to her in terms of Eve before the fall, and so an undiscerning reader might assume that what is predicated in paradisiacal terms of Mary *after* the Incarnation equally applied to all her life before—it is at this stage that one arrives at what I am calling the "static" viewpoint. It is this static view that essentially underlies the various apocryphal lives of Mary; it also seems to me to be the basis for some of the less fortunate trends in Western Marian devotion.

Linked with this static view is a tendency, frequently to be observed in the history of religions, to take as literal truth what was originally intended to be the language of the symbol, poetry, metaphor, midrash, myth (in the good sense of the word), or whatever one may like to call it. This is basically a fundamentalist approach, and one that fossilizes typology, using it as a basis for creating fixed dogmas, whereas the typological approach to the Bible as found in the Syriac (and of course other) Fathers is essentially a fluid one, refusing to be contained by dogmatic statements on the one hand, or considerations of modern biblical scholarship and its findings on the other. Indeed, one wonders whether this approach does not offer the openings of a *via tertia* for twentieth-century Western Christianity in its dilemma when faced with the liberal critical approach to the Bible that to many seems purely destructive, on the one side, and a distastefully fundamentalist approach on the other. It must of course be realized that typological exegesis can never, by its very nature, lay any claims to scientific objectivity, seeing that it belongs to a completely different mode of thought.

The parallels and contrasts between Eve and Mary are drawn in great detail by Syriac poets, and the love of symmetry has resulted in the appearance of a number of purely "mythological" elements, such as the quaint idea of Mary's conceiving through her ear, mentioned earlier, the object being to provide a contrast with Eve's disobedience through listening to the serpent, sin being pictured as entering through her ear, like poison, as the serpent spoke.

Another recurrent piece of imagery, and one of some importance is that of the "robe of glory." According to widespread Syriac tradition (probably of Jewish origin), Adam and Eve were stripped of their original "robes of glory" when they were expelled from the Garden of Eden. With the coming of Christ, however, the "robe of glory" is restored for mankind, in the sacrament of Baptism. Mary's essential role in this is once again stressed by Jacob:

> The second Eve gave birth to Life, among mortals; she wiped clean the bill of debt incurred by Eve her mother. The child (Mary) gave her hand to help her aged mother (Eve), who lay prostrate; she raised her up from the fall that the serpent had effected. It was the daughter (Mary) who wove the robe of glory and gave it to her father (Adam), who then covered his body that had been naked ever since the affair of the tree. (B. 616)

As we shall see later on in another connection, this robe of glory is essentially a symbol of Baptism; Adam, according to legend, was buried on Golgotha, and there he was baptized in the water and blood that flowed from the side of Christ (Jn 19.34).

Although not directly relevant to our theme, it might be added that the imagery of the debt (taken from Colossians 2.14) in the passage quoted above was also extremely popular, and in turn gave rise to all kinds of what can best be described as "documentary" imagery. Thus, for example, to contrast with the document of debt given by Satan to Eve, Gabriel is commonly depicted as bearing a "royal missive" containing the message of the Annunciation. It was not for nothing that Aramaic had been the chancery language of the Achaemenid empire.

Woven into this basic Eve-Mary typology one finds numerous logical extensions of the initial contrasted equation between Eve and Mary. I shall dwell here momentarily on one of these. Once Adam and Eve had been expelled, the entrance to Paradise was guarded, according to the biblical account (Gen 3.24), by a cherub with a revolving sword. It is Mary who, by giving birth to Christ, removes this obstacle. In Jacob's words:

> Through Mary the path to Eden, that had been shut, was trod again; the serpent fled, and men could pass over to God. Through Mary the cherub turned aside his sword, to guard no more the Tree of Life [i.e., Christ], which had now given itself over to be eaten. (B. 637)

Now this sword of Genesis 3.24 was very frequently connected typologically by Syriac writers with the lance that pierced Christ's side in John 19.34 (a single Syriac word is often employed for both weapons), and the water and blood that issued from the pierced side were regularly interpreted in a sacramental sense—Baptism and Eucharist—in other words, just another aspect of the return to Paradise. Mary and the sacraments are thus pictured in virtually identical roles, and the same "equation," if one can call it such, will be found if one considers the typological relationship (equally commonly found) between Adam's rib and Christ's side, where Adam's rib giving birth to Eve is contrasted with Christ's side "giving birth" to the sacraments. We have already seen how Jacob also contrasts the first half (i.e., Adam:Eve) with Mary's giving birth to Christ, and so this accordingly becomes the theoretical equivalent to Christ's side giving birth to the sacraments. Such a typological pattern is never, of course, given explicitly by Jacob, but its implicit presence is characteristic of the great flexibility in the *communicatio typorum*, if I may so call it, that one finds in these Syriac poets. We shall see very much the same sort of thing in connection with the last topic I want to deal with: Mary and Baptism.

To Ephrem, Christ's Birth from Mary as well as from the Father was an indication that man, too, requires a second birth—that is, at Baptism—and once again the chiastic structure of this piece of typology gives the artistic symmetry that the Syriac poets loved so much. A number of factors suggested these links. In the first place one must remember that in Ephrem's day Christ's Nativity and Baptism were still celebrated on the same day (our Epiphany), and that, at least in some localities, Baptisms were held at this time, rather than at Easter. The links were further suggested by the characteristically Syriac imagery of the baptismal waters as a womb, and the fact that Christ's presence in the Jordan was widely regarded in the early Syriac-speaking Church as having potentially sanctified all baptismal water. The parallelism thus created between Christ in His mother's womb and in the "womb" of the Jordan water leads Ephrem to regard Christ's very presence in Mary's womb as the equivalent of *her* Baptism:

> The Light settled on Mary, as on an eye; it purified her mind, it cleansed her understanding, it washed her thought, it made her virginity shine. The river in which Christ was baptized conceived Him again symbolically, the damp womb of the water conceived Him in purity, and bore Him in holiness, made Him rise up in glory. In the pure womb of the river you should recognize the daughter of man, who conceived without the aid of man, and gave birth as a virgin, and who brought up, through a gift, the Lord of that gift. *(H. Eccles. 36.2–4)*

It will be noticed here that, to Ephrem, the whole of Christ's incarnate life, from the Nativity to the Ascension, is gathered up in His Baptism, thus explaining the apparent reversal of time in Mary's Baptism. Elsewhere Ephrem makes the point more explicitly, addressing Christ:

> You have given birth to Your own mother in the second birth that comes from water. *(H. Nativ. 16.9)*

And a little later on he says the same thing in terms of the imagery of the "robe of glory," touched on above (Mary speaks):

> The Son of the Most High came and dwelt in me, and I became His mother. As I gave birth to Him—His second Birth—so too He gave birth to me a second time. He put on His mother's robe—His body; I put on His glory. (*H. Nativ.* 16.11)

Further connections between Mary and Baptism are provided by the imagery of Christ as fire, particularly common in Ephrem:

> Fire and Spirit are in the womb of her who bore You, Fire and Spirit are in the river in which You were baptized, Fire and Spirit are in our Baptism, and in the Bread and Cup is Fire and the Holy Spirit. (*H. Fid.* 10.17)

Ephrem's picture of Mary's Baptism is extended by Jacob of Serug in a curious passage, where he regards the Baptism of John the Baptist as having taken place in his mother Elizabeth's womb, on the occasion of Mary's visit:

> Mary's greeting fulfilled the priest's role there: Elizabeth's was like a womb of Baptism; the Son of God sent the Spirit from His own essence, and the child John was baptized by the Holy Spirit while still in his mother's womb. (B. 646–7)

With this somewhat bizarre picture we may draw to an end. The important thing to remember, however, when faced with passages such as this, is that the Syriac poets provide this wealth of phantasmagoric imagery and this kaleidoscope of "mythological" pictures as contemplative aids toward a deeper appreciation and understanding of the mysteries that surround the Incarnation. To take them at their face value would be to misunderstand them completely and totally.

If one were to summarize the attitudes toward Mary as exemplified in early Syriac literature, I think it would be true to say that she is always regarded in relationship to the Incarnation, and never *in vacuo*. In Orthodox icons the Virgin is normally depicted with the incarnate Christ in her arms, symbolic of her role of cooperation with the divine economy; although the Syriac-speaking churches in fact do not make great use of icons, this iconographical tradition admirably exemplifies their Christocentric approach. And Mary's relationship to the Holy Spirit is always clear cut: the Holy Spirit is essentially the Sanctifier, while Mary is the sanctified, par excellence. This relationship of cooperation receives its perfect expression in the words of the Nicene creed, in their eastern form: "... born of the Holy Spirit *and* Mary the Virgin."

Sebastian Brock

Life of Jacob of Serug

Holy Mar Jacob, teacher, flute of the Holy Spirit and harp of the faithful Church! He was from the village of Curtam, which is near the Euphrates. He was born of the vows of faithful but barren parents. When he was three years old, he was presented in the Church by his mother on one of the festivals of our Lord. At the time of the Liturgy, at the descent of the Holy Spirit on the Mysteries, the saint got down from the side of his mother and broke through the crowd and went to the altar and received three "handfuls" of the Holy Spirit. From that time he began to utter homilies and treatises. Immediately the bishops heard, and they arose and came to him that they might examine him. They commanded him to recite a treatise concerning the chariot that Ezekiel had seen. So he began to recite: O Exalted One who sit on the heavenly chariot . . . Then they commanded that he deliver his teaching to the assembly in writing. And he began to set down homilies and treatises for the assembly when he was twenty-two years old. Afterward he became bishop of the town of Serug when he was sixty-seven and a half, which was the year 830 of the Greeks and 519 after the coming of Christ.

Then when he had filled the Church with the doctrine of salvation and had deluged the whole earth with his teaching and with his excellent interpretations, he departed to his Lord and was buried with honor in the town of Serug in the year 833, on the twenty-ninth of November. All the years of his life were seventy: sixty-seven and a half before he became bishop and two and a half years while he was bishop.

Concerning the Blessed Virgin Mother of God, Mary

O Beneficent One, whose door is open to evil ones and to
  sinners,
Grant me to enter and see Your beauty while I marvel.

O treasure of blessings, from which even the unjust are
  satiated,
may I be nourished by You because You are entirely life for
  him who partakes of You.

Cup that inebriate the soul with Your draught, and it forgets
  its sufferings;
may I drink from You, become wise in You, and recite Your
  story.

O You, who ungrudgingly magnify our unworthy race,
my word extols beautiful things with Your psalms.

Son of Greatness, who became a little child,
grant my feeble self to speak concerning Your greatness.

Son of the Most High, who wanted to be with earthly beings,
may my word be raised on high and speak to You.

615 You, our Lord, are an eloquent word that is full of life
and a great discourse that gives riches to the one who hears it.

Everyone who speaks about You is speaking because of You,
since You are word and rational mind and conscience.

1

Neither the thoughts of the soul stir without You,
nor do words move the lips except in You.

Lips give no sound without Your command,
nor is there hearing in the ear without Your favor.

Behold, Your riches are lavished on those far and near;
Your door is opened for the good and the evil ones to come
    into You.

Everyone is rich in You, and You are enriching everyone
    without measure;
May [my] discourse be enriched by You with beauty, and may
    it speak to You.

Son of the Virgin, grant me to speak about Your Mother,
while I acknowledge that the word concerning her is too
    exalted for us.

The Mystery[1] of Mary

A wonderful discourse has now moved me to speak;
You who are discerning, lovingly incline the ear of the soul!

The story of Mary stirs in me, to show itself in wonder;
You, wisely, prepare your minds!

The holy Virgin calls me today to speak of her;
let us purge our hearing for her luminous tale, lest it be
    dishonored.

Second heaven, in whose womb the Lord of heaven dwelt
and shone forth from her to expel darkness from the lands.

---

[1] "Mystery" is a favorite term of Jacob. He wants to lead beyond speculation to an attitude of prayer and wonder at the mysteries and marvels of the Lord. For the symbolic quality of Syriac exegetical poetry, see Sebastian P. Brock, "The Poet as Theologian," *Sobornost* 7 (1977): 243–50.

616 Blessed of women, by whom the curse of the land[2] was
    eradicated,
and the sentence henceforth has come to an end.

Modest, chaste, and filled with beauties of holiness,
so that my mouth is inadequate to speak a word concerning her.

Daughter of poor ones, who became mother of the Lord of Kings
and gave riches to a needy world that it might live from Him.

Ship that bore treasure and blessings from the house of the
    Father
and came and poured out riches on our destitute earth.

Good field that, without seed, gave a sheaf[3]
and grew a great yield while being unploughed.

Second Eve who generated Life among mortals,
and paid and rent asunder that bill of Eve, her mother.

Maiden who gave help to the old woman who was prostrate;
she raised her from the fall where the serpent had thrust her.

Daughter who wove a garment of glory[4] and gave it to her
    father;
he covered himself because he was stripped naked among the
    trees.

[2]Gen 3.17–18.

[3]"Good field," Mt 13.23; "sheaf," Lev 23.10–11.

[4]Aphrahat says of Christ, "He is the garment and robe of glory which all the
victorious put on." See Demonstration 14 in Robert Murray, *Symbols of Church and
Kingdom: A Study in Early Syriac Tradition* (Cambridge: Cambridge University Press,
1975). The "garment of glory" is lost at the fall, recovered at Baptism, while awaiting
the final aspect of eschatological clothing. For a survey of this important topic of
Syriac literature, see Sebastian P. Brock, "Clothing Metaphors as a Means of Theological Expression in Syriac Tradition," in *Typus, Symbol, Allegorie bei den östlichen
Vätern und ihren Parallelen im Mittelalter: internationales Kolloquium, Eichstätt 1981,*
ed. Margot Schmidt and Carl-Friedrich Geyer, Eichstätter Beiträge 4 (Regensburg:
Verlag Friedrich Pustet, 1982), 11–40. Examples of this metaphor may also be found
in Jewish literature, see Gershom G. Scholem, *Jewish Gnosticism, Merkabah Mysticism, and Talmudic Tradition* (New York: Jewish Theological Seminary, 1960), 56–64.

Virgin who without marital union marvelously became a
mother,
a mother who remained without change in her virginity.

Fair palace that the King built and entered and dwelt in it;
the doors were not opened before Him when He was going
out.[5]

Maiden who became like the heavenly chariot[6]
and solemnly carried that Mighty One, bearing Creation.[7]

617 Bride who conceived although the bridegroom had never
been seen by her;
she gave birth to a baby without her coming to the place of
His Father.

How can I form an image of this most fair one,
with ordinary colors whose mixtures are not suitable for her?

The image of her beauty is more glorious and exalted than my
composition;
I do not dare let my mind depict the form of her image.

It is easier to depict the sun with its light and its heat
than to tell the story of Mary in its splendor.

Perhaps the rays of the sphere can be captured in pigments,
but the tale concerning her is not completely told by those
who preach.

If anyone ventures, in what order can he describe her
and with what class must he mix to tell it with?

With virgins, with saints, with the chaste?
With married women, with mothers, or with handmaids?

[5]Ezek 44.2.
[6]Ezek 1.
[7]Col 1.17; Heb 1.3.

Behold the body of the glorious one carries tokens of virginity
  and milk,
perfect birth yet sealed womb; who is equal to her?

While it seems that she is in the company of maidens,
I see her, like a handmaid, giving milk to the Lad.

While I hear that Joseph her husband dwells with her,
I behold her who is not joined in conjugal union.

618 While I seek to reckon her in the order of virgins,
behold, the sound of birth pangs striking her comes to me.

Because of Joseph, I think to call her a married woman,
but I believe that she has not been known by any mortal.

I see her who bears the son of a fertile mother,
yet it seems to me that she belongs in the order of virgins.

She is virgin and mother and wife of a husband yet unmated;
how may I speak if I say that she is incomprehensible?

Love moves me to speak of her, which is proper,
but the height of her discourse is too difficult for me; what will I do?

I will cry openly that I have not been fit nor am I yet,
and I will return because of love that I might recount her story
  that is exalted.

Only love does not reproach when speaking,
because its way is pleasing and enriches the one who hears it.

With wonder I will speak of Mary while I stand in awe,
because the daughter of earthly beings has ascended to such a
  high rank.[8]

---

[8]Here begins a long discourse on humility as the basis of Christian life with Mary as paradigmatic. A similar emphasis is found in Aphrahat, Demonstration 9. See *Aphraate le Sage Persan. Les exposés,* trans. M. J. Pierre, Sources Chrétiennes 349 (Paris: Editions du Cerf, 1988). See also *Liber Graduum,* ed. M. Kmosko, Patrologia Syriaca 3 (Paris: Firmin-Didot, 1926), cols. 212; 624–625.

How did grace itself bend down the Son to her,
or was she so beautiful that she became Mother to the Son of
  God?

That God descended on earth by grace is manifest,
and since Mary was very pure, she received Him.

619 He looked on her humility and her gentleness and her purity,
and dwelt in her because it is easy for Him to dwell with the
  humble.

"On whom will I gaze except the gentle and humble?"[9]
He looked on and dwelt in her because she was humble
  among those who are born.

Even she herself said that He looked on her lowliness and
  dwelt in her,[10]
because of this she shall be extolled, for she was so.

Humility is total perfection,
so that when man first beholds God, then he behaves humbly.

For Moses was humble,[11] a great one among all men;
God went down to him on the mountain in revelation.

Again humility is seen in Abraham,[12]
for although he was just, he called himself dust and ashes.

Again also John was humble because he was proclaiming
that he was not worthy to loose the sandals of the Bridegroom,
  his Lord.[13]

By humility, the heroic in every generation have been pleasing,
because it is the great way by which one draws near to God.

[9]Cf. Is 57.15; 66.2.
[10]Cf. Lk 1.48.
[11]Cf. Num 12.3; Ex 3.11.
[12]Cf. Gen 18.27.
[13]Cf. Mk 1.7; Lk 3.16; Jn 1 .27.

But no one on earth was brought low like Mary,
and from this it is manifest that no one was exalted like her.

In proportion to lowliness, the Lord also bestows
manifestation;
He made her His mother and who is like her in humility?

620 If there were another, purer and gentler than she,
in this one He would dwell and that one renounce, so as not to
dwell in her.

And if there were a soul [more] splendid and holy,
rather than hers, He would choose this one and forsake that
one.

God's Choice of Mary

Our Lord descending to earth beheld all women;
He chose one for Himself who among them all was pleasing.

He searched her and found humility and holiness in her,
and limpid impulses and a soul desirous of divinity.

And a pure heart and every reckoning of perfection,
because of this He chose her, the pure and most fair one.

He descended from His place and dwelt within the glorious
one among women,[14]
because for her there was not a companion comparable to her
in the world.

[14]"Dwelt within," *aggen,* Luke 1.35 has roots in Targumim signifying divine intervention. Eventually the term was used in Syriac anaphoras. Also later spiritual writers like Isaac of Nineveh used *aggen* to speak of transformation. See Sebastian P. Brock, "Passover, Annunciation and Epiclesis: Some Remarks on the Term *aggen* in the Syriac Versions of Lk 1:35," *Novum Testamentum* 24.3 (1982): 222–233. For the relationship of the Targum tradition to the Syriac Bible, the Peshitta, see Sebastian P. Brock, "Jewish Traditions in Syriac Sources," *Journal of Jewish Studies* 30 (1979): 212–32.

She alone is humble, pure, limpid, and without blemish,
so that she was deemed worthy to be His mother and not
 another.

He observed her, how exalted and pure from evil,
nor stirs in her an impulse inclined to lust.

And she allows no thought for luxury,
nor worldly conversation that causes cruel harm.

Desire for worldly vanity does not burn in her,
nor is she occupied with childish things.

He saw that there was not like her, nor equal to her in the
 world,
then He took her as mother that He might suck pure milk
 from her.

621 She was a person of discernment, full of the love of God,
because our Lord does not dwell where there is no love.

When the great King desired to come to our place,
He dwelt in the purest shrine of all the earth because it pleased
 Him.

He dwelt in a spotless womb that was adorned with virginity,
and with thoughts that were worthy of holiness.

She was most fair both in her nature and in her will,
because she was not sullied with displeasing desires.

From her childhood, she stood firm in unblemished
 uprightness;
she walked in the way without offenses.

Her original nature was preserved with a will for good things
because there were always tokens of virginity in her body and
 holy things in her soul.

This deed that took place in her gave me power
to speak these things concerning her ineffable beauty.

Because she became Mother of the Son of God, I saw and
    firmly believed
that she is the only woman in the world who is entirely pure.

From when she knew to distinguish good from evil,[15]
she stood firm in purity of heart and in integrity of thoughts.

She did not turn aside from the justice that is in the Law,
and neither carnal nor bodily desire disturbed her.

622 From her childhood, impulses of holiness stirred within her,
and in her excellence, she increased them with great care.

The Lord was always set before her eyes;
on Him she was gazing, so that she might be enlightened by
    Him, and delighted in Him.

Because He saw how pure she was and limpid her soul,
He wanted to dwell in her since she was free from evils.

Since a woman like her had never been seen,
an amazing work was done in her that is the greatest of all.

A daughter of men was sought among women;
she was chosen who was the fairest of all.

The Holy Father wanted to make a mother for His Son,
but He did not allow that she be His mother because of His choice.

Maiden, full of beauty hidden in her and around her,
and pure of heart that she might see the mysteries that had
    come to pass in her.

This is beauty, when one is beautiful of one's own accord;
glorious graces of perfection are in her will.

[15]Is 7.16.

However great be the beauty of something from God,
it is not acclaimed if freedom is not present.

The sun is beautiful but it is not praised by spectators,
because it is known that its will does not give it light.

623 Whoever is beautiful of his own accord and possesses beauty,
on this account he is truly acclaimed if he is beautiful.

Even God loves beauty that is from the will;
He praises a good will whenever this has pleased Him.

Now this Virgin whom, behold, we speak of her story
by means of her good will, she was pleasing and was chosen.

He was descending to become man by the daughter of man;
because she was pleasing, she was chosen that He might be
    from her.

And since His grace is greater than that of all who are born,
the beauty of Mary shall be much extolled because she was
    His Mother.

By her humility, by her purity, by her uprightness, and by her
    good will,
she was pleasing and was chosen for Him.

If another had pleased more than she, He would have chosen
    that one,
for the Lord does not respect persons since He is just and
    right.[16]

If there had been a spot in her soul or a defect,
He would have sought for Himself another mother in whom
    there is no blemish.

This beauty, which is the most pure of all beauties,
exists in the one who possesses it by means of a good will.

[16]2 Chr 19.7; Acts 10.34; Gal 2.6.

On account of this it is right that everyone marvel at the
    glorious one,
because of how much she was pleasing, even to the Lord
    choosing her as Mother.

She was pleasing as much as it is given nature to be beautiful,
but she did not reach this measure by her will.

624   Hitherto she strove with human virtue,
    but that God should shine forth from her was not of her own doing.

As far as the just ones drew near to God,
the most fair one drew near by the virtue of her soul.

But that the Lord shone from her bodily,
His grace it is, may He be praised because of so much mercy!

The beauty of Mary is beyond measure,
because another who is greater than she has not arisen in all
    the world.

From this time forth let us give what is due to the Lord,
because He has shed His grace on creatures without measure.

Understand the former of the Son for whom all the ages are
    not sufficient,
and now this of Mary whom among mothers there is no one
    greater than she.

She was made pure like John[17] and like Elisha,
like Elias and like Melchizedek, who were renowned.

She ascended to this degree of these heights in beauty,
so she was chosen to be the Mother of the Son of the Holy One.

She drew near to the limit of virtue by her soul;
so, that grace that is without limit dwelt in her.

---

[17]Cf. Lk 1.15.

She who was full of the beauty of holiness looked to the Lord;
He sought to dwell solemnly in her pure womb.

625 Then He sent a Watcher[18] from the heavenly legions,
that he might bring the good tidings to the blessed one, most
    fair.

Gabriel, the great chief of the hosts, descended;
he went down to her as he had been sent from God.[19]

Because she alone was worthy of the great mystery
that was rich in divine revelations.

With prayers and in limpidity[20] and in simplicity,
Mary received that spiritual revelation.

She being holy and standing in wonder in God's presence,
her heart was poured forth with love in prayer before Him.

She was in prayer, as also Daniel was in prayer,[21]
when this same Watcher of light descended to him.

While Zechariah the priest was standing in the Sanctuary to
    pray before God,
the Watcher visited him.[22]

This maiden who was capable of receiving a more important
    revelation,
she was in prayer when she received the Watcher who had
    descended.

---

[18]"Watcher," a term used for angels in the Syriac tradition.

[19]Lk 1.26.

[20]"Limpidity," *shafyuta*, is rooted in Targumic literature. In early Syriac writers the term indicates a receptivity to revelation. See Sebastian P. Brock, "The Prayer of the Heart in Syriac Tradition," *Sobornost* n.s. 4 (1982): 135–36. In later Syriac literature *shafyuta* is often used concerning prayer. See Gabriel Bunge, "Le Lieu de Limpidité," *Irenikon* 55 (1982): 7–18.

[21]Dan 9.20–23.

[22]Lk 1.11–13.

Prayer that is limpid conspires with God;
it speaks to Him, listens to Him, and confides in Him.

The Descent of the Angel

The Watcher had descended while Mary was standing in
    prayer;
he gave her the greeting that was sent to her from the Most
    High:[23]

"Peace to you Mary, blessed one, our Lord is with you;
blessed are you and blessed is the Fruit of your virginity."

626 Then when she heard it, she was prudently reflecting
on what might be the cause of this unusual greeting.

The Watcher said, "Do not be afraid, O full of mercy,
the Lord has chosen you that in your virginity you might be
    His Mother.

"Behold from this time you will solemnly conceive;
you will give birth to the great One whose kingdom is without
    end."

Mary said, "How then will what you say happen
since man has never been known to me; how will I bring
    forth?

"You have announced a Son to me but I am not conscious of
    marital union;
I have heard of nativity, but I see no marriage."

That moment was full of wonder when Mary was standing,
conversing in argument with Gabriel.

One humble daughter of poor folk and one angel
met each other and spoke of a wonderful tale.

[23]Lk 1.26ff.

A pure Virgin and a fiery Watcher spoke with wonder:
a discourse that reconciled dwellers of earth and heaven.

One woman and the prince of all the hosts
had made an agreement for the reconciliation of the whole
world.

The two had sat between heavenly beings and earthly ones;
they spoke, attended to, and made peace for those who were
wroth.

627 Maiden and Watcher met each other and conversed in
argument on the matter
until they abolished the conflict between the Lord and
Adam.

That great strife that occurred amidst the trees[24]
came up for discussion, and it all came to an end; there was
peace.

An earthly being and a heavenly one spoke with love;
the struggle between the two sides ceased, and they were at
peace.

Eve's Legacy Overturned

The evil time that had killed Adam was changed;
another good time came in which he would be raised.

Instead of that serpent, Gabriel arose to speak;
instead of Eve, Mary began to consent.

Instead of the treacherous one who brought death by the tale
he set forth,
the truthful one arose to announce life by the tidings that he
brought.

---

[24]Gen 3.1–7.

Instead of the mother who wrote among the trees what she
     owed,
the daughter paid all the debts of Adam, her father.

Eve and the serpent with the Watcher and Mary were
     transmuted;
that affair was put right that had become distorted from the
     beginning.

See how Eve's ear inclines and hearkens
to the voice of the deceiver when he hisses deceit to her.

But come and see the Watcher instilling salvation into Mary's ear
and removing the insinuation of the serpent from her and
     consoling her.

That building that the serpent pulled down, Gabriel built up;
Mary rebuilt the foundation that Eve broke down in Eden.

628 Two virgins who received the message from two messengers;
two by two, generations were sent forth, one against another.

Satan sent a secret to Eve by means of the serpent;
the Lord sent the good tidings to Mary by means of the
     Watcher.

A confutation of the discourse that the serpent spoke,
Gabriel made against the evil one in the ear of Mary on
     account of Eve.

He renewed the discourse but refuted the arguments with his
     words;
he spoke the truth and removed all falsehood.

A virgin was beguiled by the mischief-maker in Eden;
her ear piped the sound of the great deception.

Instead of this virgin another was chosen;
truth was spoken to her in her ear from the Most High.

By the door that death entered, by it entered life
and loosened the great bond that the evil one had bound
    there.

Where sin and death had abounded from the beginning,
also grace was made to abound that would vivify Adam.[25]

The serpent did not salute Eve when speaking to her,
for there is no peace in the way that is full of death.

He chanted deception to her, fanned falsehood upon her,
on her virginity poured forth evil counsels and deceitful
    answers.

629 Enmity, conspiracy to kill, and desire for blood,
he placed in the midst of the discourse that he had delivered
    to the house of Adam.

The Watcher sent by the Son, went and stood firm against
    these things;
to Mary he brought the tidings of salvation from God.

He saluted her, implanted life in her, proclaimed peace to her;
he encountered her with love and brought to an end the
    former things.

That wall of iniquity that the serpent had built then,
by His descent the Son of God broke it down that it might
    never again be restored.

When He descended, He broke down the hedge that was
    placed between the sides,
that there might be peace between dwellers on earth and in
    heaven.

On this account, the Watcher had saluted Mary
as a pledge of great peace for the whole world.

[25]Rom 5.20–21.

"Hail Mary, our Lord is with you," he was saying to her,
"you will conceive and bear a Son in your virginity."

She said to him, "How will this be as you say,
since I am a virgin and there is no fruit of virgins?"

In that moment it was very necessary to question,
so that the mystery of the Son dwelling in her might be
    explained to her.

Mary inquired in order that we might learn from the angel
concerning that conception that is a sublime matter beyond
    understanding.

Behold how most fair is Mary to the one who beholds her,
and how loveable these things of hers to the ones who are
    capable of discerning.

630 This one inquires that she might learn from him about her
    conception,
because it was hers and for the profit of the one who listens to
    her.

Eve had not questioned the serpent when he led her astray,
she who by her will kept silent and firmly believed the
    treachery.

The latter maiden heard truth from the faithful one,
nevertheless in this way she had sought out an explanation.

The former heard of becoming a goddess from a tree,[26]
but she did not say, "How will what you mention ever
    happen?"

The Watcher told this one that she would conceive the Son of
    God,
but she did not accept it until she was well informed.

[26]Gen 3.5.

That she in her person would ascend to the divine rank,
the virgin wife of Adam did not doubt the liar.

To this one who would bear the Son of God it was told,
but she inquired, sought, investigated, learned, and then kept
   silent.

See now how much more beautiful is the latter than the
   former;
because of her beauty, the Lord chose her and made her His
   Mother.

It was easy for her to keep silence and easy also to ask
   questions;
by her discernment she learned the truth from the angel.

As reprehensible as Eve was by her deed, so Mary was
   glorious;
and as the folly of this one, so that one's wisdom is shown up.

631 As much as the former is despicable because of that affair,
so the latter has no need to be ashamed by the matter of the
   Son.

As much as the former is foolish, the latter is wise to the one
   who understands,
for whatever that one owed, this one repaid.

By that former the fall, by the latter resurrection for all our
   race;
sin by Eve, but righteousness from within Mary.

By Eve's silence, guilt and the fouling of a name;
by Mary's discourse, life and light with victory.

She answered the Watcher, "How will what you tell me take
   place?"
He began explaining the way of the Son and His descent
   within her:

"The Holy Spirit will come to you with solemnity,
and the Power of the Most High will overshadow you, O most
   blessed one."[27]

Here all speech of the tongue is superfluous;
one does not speak except with the wonder of faith.

This matter requires powers of the mind more sublime than
   usual;
it requires merciful love to speak of it without dispute.

A search for salvation in the word of the Watcher!
Why ever was it necessary for the Holy Spirit to come before
   the Only-Begotten?

First the Spirit and then the Power dwelt in the pure one,
as he said to her, "The Spirit will come and the Power will
   descend."

The Power of the Most High is the Son who [comes] from the
   Most High,
that One who dwelt in her that He might come to birth in the
   flesh.

632 He is the Messiah, the Power of the Father, as it is written;
before this the Holy Spirit came within Mary.

   In this way, the Watcher announced to her that he had come
      from the house of the Father:
   "The Spirit will come and then the Power of the Most High
      will descend."

---

[27]Lk 1.35. It is important here to note the differentiation between the role of the Holy
Spirit and that of the Power that is the Word. See Sebastian P. Brock, *The Holy Spirit in
the Syrian Baptismal Tradition,* Syrian Churches Series 9 (Kottayam, India: St Ephrem
Ecumenical Research Institute [SEERI], 1979), 4.

The Descent of the Holy Spirit

Indeed, the Holy Spirit came to Mary,
to let loose from her the former sentence of Eve and Adam.

He sanctified her, purified her, and made her blessed among
women;
He freed her from that curse of sufferings on account of Eve,
her mother.[28]

She was summoned that she might be the Mother of the Son
of God;
the Holy Spirit had sanctified her and so dwelt within her.

The Spirit freed her from that debt
that she might be beyond transgression when He solemnly
dwelt in her.

He purified the Mother by the Holy Spirit while dwelling in
her,
that He might take from her a pure body without sin.

Lest the body with which He clothed Himself according to
nature be sullied,
He purified the Virgin by the Holy Spirit and then dwelt in
her.

The Son of God wanted to be related to her,
and first He made her body without sin.

The Word had descended that He might become flesh;
on this account, by the Spirit He purified the one from whom
He had become flesh,

633 so that He might become like us in everything when He
descended,
except for this: that His pure body is without sin.

[28]Cf. Gen 3.16.

He, God, wanted to be like a son of man;
by the Spirit, He purified one Virgin and made her His
 Mother,

so that He might become a second Adam from God for the
 world,[29]
to give assistance to that first one whom the serpent had
 brought low;

that when He entered to make judgement with the prince of
 the world,[30]
in man He might not find sin, which opens the door to death.

The Son of Man, while not being subject to judgement,
He, Himself God, goes out into the world from the daughter
 of man.

On this account, that holy one of renown and most blessed
 one,
the pure Virgin, He sanctified with the Spirit.

He made her pure, limpid, and blessed
as that Eve, before the serpent spoke with her.

He bestowed on her that first grace that her mother had,
until she ate from the tree that was full of death.

The Spirit who came made her like Eve of old,
though she did not hear the counsel of the serpent nor his
 hateful speech.

In that condition where Eve and Adam were placed,
before they sinned, He placed her and then descended in her.

That adoption of sons that our father Adam had,
He gave to Mary by the Holy Spirit, while dwelling in her.

[29]I Cor 15.45.
[30]Cf. Jn 12.31; 14.30.

634 As our father generated our mother without marital union,
     she also generated because she was as Adam before he sinned.

     The Holy Spirit, who had blown on Adam's face and generated
          Eve,
     she also received and gave birth to a Son.

     That purity that was in Adam, Mary also acquired
     by the Spirit who came, and she gave birth without impulse of
          lust.

     Without marital union, Adam had generated the mother of
          life;
     he prefigured the Birth of the One who indeed is the fountain
          of life, our Lord.

     Formerly, then, He had known them and had represented
          them,
     Eve and Adam, in the image of His Only-Begotten Son.

     Adam chastely generated the virgin, Eve;
     he called her by the name, mother of life,[31] and so he was a
          prophet.

     Because from her, by the second Birth,[32] life shines forth to
          the world,
     and in her virginity, she also brings forth the Son of God.

     In Adam's prophecy, our Lord was prefigured who indeed is life;
     and His mother was the Virgin Mary.

     He named Eve, the mother of all life, and prophesied,
     because she brings forth to us life—our Lord who is Jesus.

[31]Cf. Gen 3.20.

[32]Christ's first birth is from the Father. His second Birth, from Mary's womb, is
her second birth and her Baptism. For Syriac writers, such as Ephrem, Christ's presence in her womb sanctifies as in the Jordan. See Sebastian P. Brock, "St. Ephrem on
Christ as Light in Mary and in the Jordan," *Eastern Churches Review* 7 (1975): 141.

Mary ascended to that purity of that birth
because the Spirit had sanctified her, and then the Son of God
  dwelt in her.

635 He sanctified her body and made her without hateful lusts,
as the virgin Eve had been until she lusted.

The sin that entered Adam's race with impulses of desire,
the Holy Spirit cast out from her when He came within her.

That increase of evil inclination[33] that the serpent effected,
He wiped from her and filled her with holiness and integrity.

He made her new, and the Lord saw that she was very
  beautiful as the first Eve;
then He descended and was embodied in her.

Because of this, the angel had said that the Spirit would come
  to Mary
before the descent of the Word to reside in her.

Blessed Mary, who by her questions to Gabriel,
taught the world this mystery that was concealed.

For if she had not asked him how it would be,
we would not have learned the explanation of the matter of
  the Son.

---

[33]"Evil inclination," Gen 6.5; 8.21; 2 Esd 4.30; cf. Rom 7.23; See the Testament of Asher in the *Testaments of the Twelve Patriarchs* (trans. H. C. Kee.), found in James H. Charlesworth, ed., *The Old Testament Pseudepigrapha,* 2 vols (New York: Doubleday, 1983–85), 1:816–18. The concept is also mentioned in the sixth century by Cyrus of Edessa; see *Six Explanations of the Liturgical Feasts by Cyrus of Edessa,* ed. W. Macomber, Corpus Scriptorum Christianorum Orientalium 156 (Louvain: Peeters Publishers, 1974), 181. "Evil inclination" as an impulse to do or say or think things contrary to the revealed will of God is amply documented in early Jewish literature, see Genesis Rabbah 4:7, 8:21, 34:10, 54:1 in *Midrash Rabbah,* trans. Harry Freedman and Maurice Simon, 10 vols (London: Soncino Press, 1951). See also Ephraim E. Urbach, *The Sages* (Jerusalem: Magnes Press, 1979), 471–83, and Etan Levine, *The Aramaic Version of the Bible* (New York: W. De Gruyter, 1988), 93–98.

The beauty of the matter that appeared openly is because of
    her;
she was the reason that it was explained to us by the angel.

By that question, the wise one became the mouth of the
    Church;
she learned that interpretation for all Creation.

For if Mary had not had sublime impulses,
she would not have arrived to speak before the Watcher.

If she had not possessed inner and outer beauty,
Gabriel also would not have answered her with eloquence.

636 She rose up to this measure on her own,
until the Spirit, that perfecter of all, came to her.

She was full of grace from God that was more exalted than all;
the Only-Begotten dwelt in her womb to renew all.

The Virgin Mary Sent by the Father

Mary appeared to us as a sealed letter,[34]
in which were hidden the mysteries of the Son and His depth.

She gave her body as a clean sheet;
the Word wrote His essence on it, corporeally.

The Son is the Word and she is the letter, as we said,
by which forgiveness was sent forth to the whole world.

She was the letter, not because she was sealed after she was
    inscribed,
but the Divinity sealed her and then wrote on her.

[34]"Sealed letter," see, Is 29.11–12; and "Odes of Solomon," see Ode 23 in Charlesworth, *Pseudepigrapha* 2:755–56. In the *Acts of Thomas* a sealed letter is sent to awaken
the soul and lead it back to its forgotten noble birth. This is very suggestive of the
mystery of the Mother of God in the history of salvation. See *Acts of Thomas,* ed.
Albertus F. J. Klijn (Leiden: E. J. Brill, 1962), 122–25.

They sealed her and inscribed her; she was also read although
    not being opened,
because the Father revealed in her mysteries more sublime
    than usual.

The Word entered and dwelt in her within the guarded seals,
tokens of virginity in her body but conception in her womb
    that is full of wonder.

With her the Father sent us tidings full of good things,
and, through her, forgiveness to all condemned for their
    bonds of sin.

By her, emancipation was sent to Adam who had been enslaved;
he became an heir and came in among the sons, as he had been.

By her, heavenly beings made reconciliation with those below,
and the sides that had been at enmity were in great peace.

637 Because of her, confusion of face was lifted from womanhood;
the reproach of all women passed away from the nations.

Because of her, the way to Eden that had been blocked was
    opened;[35]
the serpent fled and men passed along it to God.

Because of her, the cherub had removed his lance that he
    might no longer guard
the Tree of Life that offered itself to those who ate it.[36]

[35]Cf. Gen 3.24.

[36]"Lance," the Syriac word used here is the same as that found in John 19.34,
suggesting important theological connections. The same word, *rumha,* is also used
very suggestively by Ephrem in his commentary on Tatian's *Diatessaron* concerning
the sword in Luke 2.35: " 'You shall cause the sword to pass': the sword which guarded
Paradise because of Eve was removed by Mary." Cited in Sebastian P. Brock, "The Mysteries Hidden in the Side of Christ," *Sobornost* 7 (1978): 462–71. See also *Saint Ephrem's
Commentary on Tatian's Diatessaron: An English Translation of Chester Beatty Syriac
MS 709 with Introduction and Notes*, trans. Carmel McCarthy, Journal of Semitic
Studies Supplement 2 (Oxford: Oxford University Press, 1993).

She gave us a sweet Fruit, full of life,
that we might eat from it and live forever with God.

The great Sun of Righteousness[37] shone forth from her,
and a glorious light that banished darkness from the region.

The Father chose her to be the mother of His Only-Begotten;
on this account, great is her blessing above those who are
    born.

Praise and Thanksgiving

"All nations henceforth will call me blessed,"
Mary said, by the light of her soul on account of her fruit.

She beheld to which high rank she had ascended,
that the world with great wonder would call her blessed.

She foresaw the future and said of it
that the peoples of the earth would call her virginity blessed.

By the Spirit she learned that her Son is the King of all the
    Gentiles;[38]
in tribute, she required a blessing from the nations.

638 Therefore, we also say "blessed" to the blessed one
whose blessing is truly more sublime than the [praises] of the
    whole world.

Blessed is she who received the Holy Spirit; He purified and
    polished her,
and He made her a temple, and the Lord Most High dwelt in
    her abode.

---

[37]Cf. Mal 4.2.
[38]"King of all the Gentiles." Syriac tradition has a strong sense of God's plan
for the salvation of the Gentiles. A good synthesis of this may be found in Murray,
Symbols of Church and Kingdom, 41–68.

Blessed is she because the great beauty of her virginity
    subsists;
her name shines valiantly forever.

Blessed is she for, by means of her, joy came to Adam's race;
through her the fallen arose who had been cast down from the
    house of the Father.

Blessed is she who is exalted above the union of marriage,
yet her face is unveiled to the beloved Child of mothers.

Blessed is she whose body was never defiled by lust;
behold, it is resplendent with the fair Fruit of her virginity.

Blessed is she in whose small and barren womb dwelt
the great One by whom the heavens are filled and are too
    small for Him.

Blessed is she who bore that Ancient One who generated
    Adam,
and by whom are made new all creatures who have become
    old.

Blessed is she who gave drops of milk from her members
to that One at whose command the waves of the great sea
    gushed forth.

Blessed is that one who carried, embraced, and caressed like a
    child
God mighty forevermore, by whose hidden power the world is
    carried.[39]

Blessed is she from whom the Savior appeared to the
    captives;
in His zeal He bound the captor and reconciled the earth.

---

[39]Col 1.17.

639 Blessed is she who placed her pure mouth on the lips of that
       One,
   from whose fire, the seraphim of fire hide themselves.[40]

   Blessed is she who nourished as a babe with pure milk
   the great breast from which the worlds[41] suck life.

   Blessed is she whose Son calls blessed all the blessed!
   Blessed is that One who solemnly appeared to us from your
       purity!

---

[40]Cf. Is 6.2. See Homily 3, n. 27, for a discussion of God as fire.
[41]I.e., spiritual and material worlds.

Concerning the Annunciation of the Mother of God

Son of God, who are the ineffable Word,
give me a word that sings Your praise abundantly.

O hidden One who willed to be manifest, manifest Yourself to
me,
that I with a loud voice may bring to manifestation Your
hidden story.

My mind is fertile, and it carries You on its thoughts;
with the mouth of the word, the voice brings You forth to the
hearers.

640 However, You have not just one birth,[1] Son of God;
but he who is going to speak of Your birth should only speak
of that other one.

The Father begot You beyond time, without a beginning,
and again the Virgin Mother bore You without explanation.

Grant to my mouth that also it bear You with psalms,
since it is easy for You to come to birth because You are
begotten.

The Father begot You and has granted that You become a child
also for us,
for, whatever belongs to the hidden Father, He has given to the
world.

[1]On the two births of Christ, see Homily 1, n 32.

The Father in His love, and by the grace that is in His nature,
sent His Son to us that in the end He might be Son also to us.

Because birth is easy to anyone who is born,
He did not withhold Him from us also, that we might bear
    Him in the flesh.

While He is born beyond time according to His essence,
at the end of time He became a Babe for us.

Behold the mouth again dares to generate Him with psalms,
and He gives Himself again that He might be offspring
    because He is generated.

He has a Father, and by His grace He has taken a mother for
    Himself;
when He was born, He descended and He dwelt in her, that
    He might be her Offspring.

He chose for Himself a virgin who was betrothed and
    preserved;
she was holy, modest, and vigilant.

He descended and dwelt in the blessed one, most fair;
her womb was sealed, her body was holy, and her soul was
    limpid.

The Mission of Gabriel

641 The revelation went out from God to the pure one
by means of Gabriel, the learned one, who teaches fine
    sayings.

The man of fire was sent from God
that he might bring the message from the house of the Father
    to the glorious one.

From the heavenly legions, the spiritual one went forth,
who had been sent from God with a hidden mystery.

He met with the maiden, greeted her, and revealed the
  mystery,
as he had been commanded by God in the heavens above.

He bowed to the Virgin, the Mother of the King, and he spoke
  with her
in the speech of the country such as she was able to receive:

"Peace be with you, full of divine splendor!
Peace to you, Mary, Mother of the Sun of Justice![2]

"Peace be upon you, castle of holy things and full of virtues,
harbor of mysteries and new ship full of riches.

"Blessed of women, peace be with you! Our Lord is with you;[3]
you have conceived, and in your virginity you have borne a
  son."

Mary listened, and wonder seized her at the words of the
  Watcher;
the message was in her ears and great trembling within her
  mind:

"My Lord, I am a virgin, and how is it that you speak to me of
  conception?
Your tale is new; speak, explain what you are saying.

"Who has sought a harvest from the land without sowing it?
Who has sought grapes on the vine without cultivating it?

642 "From a virgin who would expect birth without marital
  union?
Tell your tale that is baffling and concealed from the intellect.

---

[2]Cf. Mal 4.2.
[3]Lk 1.28ff.

"How will what you say come to pass, as you say it?[4]
Either explain it to me, or it will not be easy for me to
   consent."

The Watcher said, "The Holy Spirit will come to you;[5]
descending, He dwells and sanctifies you in your virginity.

"He loosens from you the curse of Eve and blesses you;
the Power of the hidden Father[6] comes and in you will be
   clothed with a body.

"You are going to beget a Babe whose kingdom will have no
   end;[7]
because He is a great King, the Son of the unsearchable God.

Elizabeth, Next of Kin

"And behold, Elizabeth, your next of kin who was sterile, is
   pregnant;
she also has marvelously conceived in her latter years."

How could the wife of the high priest be a kinswoman of
   Mary,[8]
being herself a Levite,[9] and Mary is of the house of David?

The tribe of Levi consisted of priests and not of kings;
that of Judah put forth kings, behold, out of David.

The tribe of kings was distant from the Levites,
but why did the Watcher call the sterile one Mary's next of
   kin?

[4]Lk 1.34.
[5]Lk 1.35.
[6]Cf. Jn 1.18; "Power" as Word, see Homily 1, n. 27.
[7]Cf. Lk 1.33.
[8]Lk 1.36.
[9]Lk 1.5.

A relation is one whose family is very near,
but that Levite was distant from the woman of Judah's tribe.

643 She was not from her tribe and not from the family of the
blessed one.
Why then was she called her kinswoman by that fiery one?

That Mary is from Judah and from the house of David,
the Book testifies in the census in which she was inscribed.

And Joseph the just one, her spouse, her kin, also of the same
race;
it is written of him that he was from that tribe of Judah.

They required him to go to Bethlehem for the census,
as there the tribe of David was inscribed.

Mary was led with him, as daughter of the same family,
because both of them were known to be of the same tribe.

But Elizabeth, the wife of the priest, daughter of Levites,
was a Levite with her husband, the high priest.

That the Watcher should deceive saying one thing instead of
another is not possible;
no, the company of Gabriel does not deceive.

So why then did he call the daughter of David
a kinswoman of the daughter of the Levites? Let us listen
willingly.

That angel is not of human nature,
but is of spiritual origin, a sublime nature.

The case of the two women fell together as far as the angel was
concerned,
so he called them kinswomen, as truly they are.

644 As tho' one might say, "You are a daughter of man, and she is a
          daughter of man;
you are a virgin, but she is truly sterile."

There is no way for a virgin to give birth,
nor is an old sterile one ever able to bring forth.

But if God commands that even sterile ones beget, and also
          virgins,
who can resist Him, or who can hinder Him?

He commands the old sterile one to bring forth, for she is your
          kinswoman;
she is also of the human race.

Also to you, daughter of man, He gave a command that in
          your virginity
you bring forth a child whose kingdom is without end.[10]

Now, friend, understand for what cause,
behold, Elizabeth was called a kinswoman of Mary.

That angel does not distinguish between one tribe and another,
but between the race of men and of angels.

As tho' one might say, "I am an angel and you are women,
and to both of you I have descended to bring good tidings.

"The Lord sent me to go down and to say that the sterile one is
          engendering,
and now He sends me to announce that the Virgin will bring
          forth.

"Behold in the sterile one, a Voice that goes forth to prepare
          the way;[11]
behold in you, the Word will arise to give life to the whole world."

[10]Cf. Lk 1.33.
[11]Cf. Lk 3.4.

Now, therefore, do not doubt what you hear about Mary
who is kinswoman of the daughter of Levites,

645 For it is not written that Mary was of the house of Levi,
nor is Elizabeth imagined to be of the house of David.

Mary is truly the daughter of David,[12]
for the Son of David is the Fruit of her flesh.

As for that "kinship," which was proclaimed by the angel,
that spiritual being simply sought to compare one woman
    with another:

"Behold Elizabeth your kinswoman has conceived a son in her
    old age!"
And Mary went to see the truth that was spoken to her.[13]

The Meeting with Elizabeth

She diligently made straight for Elizabeth
to see there the great wonder concerning the new
    conception.

Mary firmly believed all that the faithful Watcher had said,
and she indeed gloriously received conception.

She went to see the old woman who was worn out but also
    pregnant,
because she firmly believed the words that she had heard from
    the angel.

The maiden and the old woman saw one another; one might
    say that
morning and evening met one another to kiss.

---

[12]Cf. Lk 1.32.

[13]On Elizabeth's prophetic role see Origen in his homily on Luke 1.39–45 in
Origen, Homilies on Luke, trans. Joseph T. Lienhard, S.J., *Fathers of the Church* 94
(Washington, DC: Catholic University of America Press, 1996).

Mary is the morning and bears the Sun of Justice,[14]
but Elizabeth is the evening who bears the star of light.[15]

The morning came and greeted the evening, its companion,
and the evening was stirred seeing the morning kiss it.

646 The young Virgin was wise and was humble;
the old woman reverenced her like a mother when she
received her.

Because the star was not able to receive the sun,
it was moved by its manifestation and began constraining to
make merry.[16]

The light of the morning met the evening darkness and roused it,
but it was not able to endure its rays.

The maiden spoke, and the child of the old woman stirred and
was astonished;
for the Word had moved the Voice to manifest himself.

The Son of the Virgin, the Ancient of Days[17] and Ancient of
the ages,
began to do a new deed among the Levites.

He anointed the babe with the Holy Spirit in the womb of his
mother,
and He gave him Baptism in the womb before birth.[18]

The greeting of Mary was spoken into the ears of the old
woman,
and the Holy Spirit was poured into the soul of the babe.

[14]Cf. Mal 4.2.
[15]Cf. Jn 5.35.
[16]Cf. Lk 1.41–44.
[17]Dan 7.22.
[18]See Ephrem in "Hymn for the Feast of the Epiphany": "It is very right that thou
shouldst baptize Me—as I bid, and shouldst not gainsay—Lo! I baptized thee within
the womb; baptize thou Me in the Jordan!" Found in NPNF² 13:286.

Thus indeed it had been announced by the angel
that the lad would be filled with the Spirit while still in the
    womb of his mother.[19]

The Son of God partaking of the Holy Spirit
had given the Spirit to that forerunner while he was in his
    mother.

Mary's greeting fulfilled the role of the priest there
while Elizabeth was like a womb of Baptism.[20]

647 The Son of God sent forth the Spirit from His essence,
and the lad was baptized by the Holy Spirit while he was still
    in his mother's womb.

At once the confined babe began preaching
to prepare the way for the King who came from the house of
    David.

A new message was heard from within the womb,
a babe who leaps and exults and hastens to prepare the way.[21]

If nature had given power to the son of Levites,
he would have spoken and announced that his Lord had come.

But because he was not able to speak in that arduous place,
he stirred up his mother that she might fulfill his office there.

And at that time the old woman began to tell the tidings
by the Holy Spirit that the Son of the maiden had infused in
    her.

Instead of John, his mother proclaimed the message,
because it was not easy for him to speak in the place where
    babies are.

---

[19]Lk 1.15.
[20]For Baptism as a spiritual "womb," see Brock, *The Holy Spirit in the Syrian Baptismal Tradition*, 84–85.
[21]Cf. Lk 1.41–44.

She raised her voice and said, "Who grants to me, to me who
    am unworthy,
that my Lord with His mother come to me?"

That new message that was heard from Gabriel;
this was heard by Elizabeth, daughter of Levites.

Mary stood, amidst the tidings that were spoken
by the angel and by the Levite, with great wonder.

648 For Gabriel was calling the Son of Mary, "Lord,"
and so also again even Elizabeth proclaimed Him, "my Lord."

Mary knew that the One whom she carried in her virginity,
He is Lord also of earthly and celestial beings.

For Gabriel was saying to her, "The Lord is with you,"[22]
and again by Elizabeth she was called "Mother of my Lord."[23]

Mary conceived the Lord of priests and of angels,
and the wife of the priest and the chief of the angels were
    witnesses to her.

For if that One whom she bore was not God,
the angel and the priest would not have called Him "Lord."

The message of the Son had begun to reveal itself,
and it was proclaimed by angels and by men.

No one but the Father perceived the mystery of the Son,
and the Father sent it to the daughter of David by means of
    Gabriel.

Only Mary learned that hidden mystery,
but she did not reveal to anyone what was spoken to her by
    the angel.

[22]Cf. Lk 1.28.
[23]Cf. Lk 1.43.

The House of Zechariah

Yet when she had come in to Elizabeth, though she was silent,
she heard the mystery revealed and spoken in the house of the
priest.

For the priests had been aware of the hidden mystery of the
Father,
that the beloved Son would be honored among the Levites.

649 Then it was mysteriously shown to the wife of the priest,
that she might speak with Mary concerning hidden things.

Also because of this, the Watcher sent the Mother of the Light
to the house of the priests, that she might be honored among
the Levites.

For Elizabeth was worthy of this mystery,
because she carried the Voice to the Word whom Mary was
bearing.

The sterile one who was full of the Holy Spirit was the harp
that sang praise in the presence of that wonderful conception.

By the finger of the Spirit, the daughter of Aaron[24] was moved
to praise the hidden one who dwelt in virginity.

The maiden and the old woman with one mind full of wonder
were spiritually enjoying their fruits.
The Voice dwells in the old woman, but the Word in the maiden;

The high priest is deprived of his word, but his mind is rich.
Zechariah was joyful, but he was not able to speak;[25]
he rejoices at Mary and her spiritual colloquy.

Zechariah chants, rejoices, praises, and is full of wonder,
then Elizabeth lifts up her voice concerning the tidings.

[24]Cf. Lk 1.5.
[25]Cf. Lk 1.20.

The Virgin abides like an ark full of mysteries;
and the house of the priest rejoices, is merry, and honors her.

They looked on her as the habitation of the Godhead;
and she was regarded by them as an ark full of fire.

650 The priest was impeded so that he could not speak,
but he was worshiping because he perceived a hidden mystery.

He enters, worships, goes out, gives praise, beckons while
    marveling;
again he indicates with his hand and lifts his eyes while being
    amazed.

Then Elizabeth, who also was full of the Holy Spirit,
marveled at all the gestures and prayers of her husband.

For she knew what he was indicating and what he was
    beseeching,
and how he bowed himself and why he was amazed, while
    marveling.

And she became a mouth for her husband who was not
    speaking
and a harp for the sounds of her baby who was making merry.

Because the Holy Spirit was in her she manifested mysteries;
she spoke and explained the rejoicing of the lad and the
    silence of his father:

"With great joy the babe leapt for joy in me," she said to Mary,
"and who has revealed to me that the babe rejoiced, but the
    Spirit."

Whether the babe rejoices or is grieved in the womb,
who can know it without the spirit of the Godhead?

But Elizabeth had been completely filled with the Holy Spirit
and by it she had perceived the rejoicing of the lad and the
   signs of his father.

She was explaining what Zechariah was seeking to do;
she was expressing what the lad was eager to say.

651 The old woman said, "Blessed are you, maiden mother Mary!
Who dwells in you, and whom have you conceived in your
   virginity?

"The old priest worships your Son, for He is his Lord;
behold he looks on you and is moved by you because of your
   Fruit.

"That altar of incense[26] that he serves in the Holy of Holies
is not greater than you, for behold in you is the Lord of
   holiness.

"When the high priest, marveling, looks on you, he is
   speechless;
he is amazed at you because the exalted Lord dwells in you.

"Because your appearance is awesome like the thick darkness
   on Mount Sinai,[27]
the old priest trembles when he looks on you.

"Also the baby whom I carry leaps for joy because of this,
because his Lord who has come[28] visited him in his mother's
   house.

"He exults with joy and compels me to fall down and adore you
who bear the Lord of priests in your virginity.

---

[26]Heb 9.4.

[27]Ex 24.15–16.

[28]The Syriac form indicates that this is possibly a variation of *Maranatha,* see
Gerhard Kittel and Gerhard Friedrich, eds., *Theological Dictionary of the New Testa-
ment*, trans. Geoffrey W. Bromiley (Grand Rapids, MI: Wm. B. Eerdmans Publishing
Co., 1967), 4:467–69.

"The enclosed babe and his old father marvel at you,
for, behold, that One whose glory fills heaven is in your womb.

"The One who forms babes in all wombs dwells in you, Mary;
because of this the babes exult and are glad in Him.

"You bear the Lord of Aaron and of Melchizedek, the high
     priest,
and concerning this, the old priest is disquieted at your
     appearance."

For three months the sublime and divine story
was being told in the house of the priest on account of Mary.

652 They were delighting in her and boasting of her and being
        watchful over her
     and honoring her and bowing in her presence and rejoicing
        with her.

They also were reading the books of the prophecy in her
     presence
and were showing her the mysteries of the Son from the
     readings.

They were encouraging her lest she doubt on account of her
     conception,
while they were narrating all that had been spoken in the
     prophecy.

Then while the old woman was meditating on Isaiah and
     reading,
she explained and showed to Mary all that had been said,

"Behold, my daughter, in the prophecy it is written that the
     virgin will conceive;
in this prophet read and understand about your conception.[29]

---

[29]Cf. Is 7.14.

"Take with you also that scroll of the prophecy
and give it to your betrothed to read all of it and to understand it.

"Will something greater than usual stir him up when he sees
    you?
Give him the inspired prophet to read!

"That by him he might understand that a virgin will conceive
    without marriage,
that the story of your conception might be clear to him when
    it is told.

"Arise, go to him! He is a just man, and he will assist you;
reveal to him your mystery, behold your Son is anxious to
    prepare your way.

"I am falling into a bed of pain and it isn't right
that I lie down and you rise up to serve.

653 "You bear the King, and I am the servant and not able
to see the Mother of the King be in dishonor before me."

Joseph the Just One

After these things, Mary went to go home
since the time had come for the daughter of Levi to bring
    forth.

Joseph received her and learned of Mary's conception;
he, the just one, was disquieted by the new aspect, and he
    wondered.

The maiden was modest and full of all holiness;
her appearance was grave and full of all humility.

Her countenance was shining, and her face was moist with
    modesty;
she was limpid, pure, and all adorned with virginity.

And what should Joseph do, the just one, who was her betrothed,
because Mary's womb indicates to him that the Babe is there?

For she was modest, dignified, and grave;
but she was also pregnant, heavy, and conspicuous.

For three months she lived in the Levite's house,
and her womb was prominent because of the Babe she was
  carrying.

That One who forms babies was formed there;[30]
He gathered together the senses of His human nature, and He
  took flesh in it.

The time was right, and His being was perfectly formed;
the Babe became flesh, and He manifested Himself there.

654 The Virgin's womb that was carrying Him was known,
and Joseph was troubled on account of the conception that he
  did not understand.

Since he was just, he did not want to put the blessed one to
  shame;
however, secretly he spoke with her concerning the deed.[31]

The Virgin also, with loud voice and uncovered face,
spoke with him, without a bride's veil.

And, with the revelations and interpretations of the prophecy,
she was urging him not to doubt on account of her
  conception.

He marveled at her while listening to her, what must he do!
The Word is great and who can believe in it without
  revelation.

---

[30]See "Hymns on the Nativity," Hymn 4, verses 169–176 in Kathleen M. McVey,
Ephrem the Syrian: Hymns, Classics of Western Spirituality (New York: Paulist Press
1989), 101–102.
    [31]Cf. Mt 1.19.

She was telling him the words that she heard from the angel,
and she was narrating to him how the priests in Judea had
   received it.

She was also reminding him what the prophets spoke;
he trembled while remaining steadfast, and he firmly believed
   everything, while hesitating.

Since he was just, he sought to put her away secretly,
so that he would not make her known nor scrutinize the
   wonderful one.

The Dream of Joseph

Because he was worthy of such divine discourse,
Gabriel, the chief of the angels, encountered him in a dream.[32]

The angel came in a nocturnal vision to speak with him
and to teach him the truth about the entirely wondrous
   conception.

In the evening he had been thinking to dissolve the betrothal,
but the Watcher came, made reconciliation in the night, and
   went away.

655 He made the document of separation with much thought
        while he was sleeping,
   but he arose in the morning, worshiping and desiring
        reconciliation.

He was sad in the evening and a spirit of doubt blew over him,
but at night he had a dream, a teacher of truth.

Gabriel descended; he comforted him and brought tidings to
   him
and explained to him all the readings of the prophecy.

---

[32]Mt 2.20–25.

The man of fire, from whose words fell burning coals,[33]
had appeared to the just one, and he trembled while believing
    and asking him questions.

"Who are you, my Lord?" The Watcher answered him saying,
"I am a servant of the Child whom Mary bears."

Joseph said, "And how many does my Lord have like you?"
The Watcher said, "An innumerable multitude, a thousand
    thousands."

Although he was quivering, Joseph was deeply moved, and he
    was full of wonder;
then he joined his hands while bowing to the glorious one.

Mary said, "Did Gabriel perhaps speak with you?
So turn your face and fix it up for it is cast down.

"What did he say to you?" He answered, "What he said to you
    he revealed to me,
that mystery that he had revealed to you while speaking to you."

Joseph took her and brought her, filled with holiness, into his
    house
while looking on her as the heavenly chariot.[34]

He was noble, and he was holy like a spiritual Melchizedek;
he was made a priest to serve the Lord of holiness.

656 The Virgin dwelt with the just one in holy awe;
the mystery was hidden from strangers, and they did not
    perceive it.

---

[33]Cf. Ezek 1.13.

[34]"Chariot," Ezek 1; 3 Enoch 24. Evidence of Merkabah mysticism can be found in
Jacob of Serug's poetry. For a historical and theological understanding of Merkabah
traditions, see P. Alexander's introduction to 3 *Enoch* in Charlesworth, *Pseudepigra-*
pha 1:225–54. Alexander also mentions possible influence of the Merkabah movement
on Syriac Christian writers, see p. 253. For the text of 3 Enoch 24 see Charlesworth,
1:308–09. All subsequent references to Enoch may be found in Charlesworth.

He did not look on the blessed one as a man on his wife;
he looked on her as the high priest looks on the Holy of Holies.

He was loving her and marveling at her and bowing to her;
he was honoring her and reverencing her and serving her.

He was regarding her like the cloud over Mount Sinai,[35]
because within her the Power of the Godhead was dwelling.

His heart was pure, and also his thoughts were holy;
he bows and gives thanks because he was deemed worthy to
    be a priest to the Son.

He was serving her like a spiritual angel,
and he was not confused by carnal thoughts.

The pure Virgin and the just man had the same intention,
for they made holiness the marriage agreement.

The chief of the angels was mediator and deemed them
    worthy
that they might dwell like angels without marital union.

In virginity and in purity and in holiness
they persevered in a marriage full of holy things.

And that hidden mystery that was told by the angel:
they were preserving it without mentioning it to strangers.

Divine Providence

657   "A mystery for me, a mystery for me!"[36]—it was a mystery to
    the father there,
and those of his house knew it but the others, no.

Because this mystery had been hidden,
a virgin was chosen who was betrothed to a just man.

[35]Ex 24.15–16.
[36]Ex 24.15–16.

Divine providence gave her in marriage;
when she was betrothed, the Son of God descended and dwelt
    in her.

For unless she had been betrothed when He dwelt in her,[37]
even her conception would have been marred and troubled.

As soon as it was known that there was a babe in her womb,
the pregnant Virgin would have been regarded as an
    adulteress.

If she revealed the hidden mystery, who would believe her,
for the virgin, in her virginity, was pregnant without a
    husband.

If, although our Lord had worked miracles, they did not
    believe in Him,
who would have believed that He was the Son of God while
    He was in the womb?

He cast out demons and gave life to the dead, yet they
    persecuted Him;
if He had revealed that He was within the womb, who would
    have given Him credence?

When He made haste above the waves of the sea, they
    despised Him,[38]
so who would have dared say that a maiden had conceived
    Him?

If Mary had revealed the divine mystery,
she would have been scorned, hated, calumniated.

658 She would have been slandered, persecuted, and stoned;
she would have been regarded as an adulteress and a liar.

---

[37]"Dwelt in," *aggen,* see Homily 1, n. 14.
[38]Mt 14.25–26; Mk 6.48; Jn 6.19.

Because of this, divine providence
had sought for her a just spouse to be her husband.

And providence desired a "head" to protect her and to shelter her
and to defend because of her conception, saying "the Child was his."

And he brought her into his house lest they reckon her among the adulteresses,
and, although he was not a husband, the just one was reckoned as her husband.

As soon as it was known that there was a babe in her womb, the Watcher commanded him,[39]
and he brought her into his house lest she suffer dishonor.

Joseph was specially chosen for that matter,
so that he might be the reputed father of our Lord at the time of His coming.

Because of this she was betrothed to him that she might repose in his name,
and that the Son of God might arise mysteriously from her.

Joseph would lend himself as the reputed father,
while recognizing who was the Father of the Son of God.

Lest scruples and doubts and anguish assail her,
without a head to guide her,

Joseph says of Mary's conception, "The conception is by me";
so gossip and ill-repute abated for the daughter of David.

659 The mystery of the Son was preserved by Joseph and completely hidden;
it was spoken of with great wonder between him and Mary.

---

[39]Cf. Mt 1.20–24.

To strangers He was said to be the son of Joseph,
both by Joseph and by Mary, who was a virgin.

While He was sitting among the teachers in the holy temple,
Mary said, "Your father and I sought You earnestly."

Before strangers she was calling Joseph His father,
and she discreetly did not reveal that she was a virgin.

But while He was sitting among the teachers and was
    questioning,[40]
He did not want to keep silent concerning her calling Joseph
    His father.

"You know that it is also right that I be in the house of My Father";
so He reproved Mary that He has a Father who is not Joseph.

Lest He keep silence, and His silence be like testimony,
He showed that He had another secret Father who is hidden.

The temple is the house of his hidden Father,
and "It is fitting that I be in the house of My Father," He said to
    Mary.

He dismissed her words concerning her calling Joseph His
    father;
He showed who is His hidden Father, and which is His house.

He did not want to be a witness to Mary that He has any father
apart from only the one God who is His Begetter.

But Mary, because of prudence, we have said,
borrowed the name of Joseph, the just one, to be His father.

660 Lest she be troubled in making a defense to the Hebrew
    women,
    at that time the Virgin called Joseph, the just one, her
    husband.

[40]Cf. Lk 2.46–49.

Joseph was appointed as a veil between her and her Son,
until the Son of God willed to reveal Himself.

For the sake of the family of Joseph, which was of the house of
David,
it was necessary that he be the spouse of the daughter of
David.

He should be her head, seeing that his name was transmitted
in the genealogies,
for in the succession of kings, no woman is inscribed.

The genealogies descended from Abraham, as well as from
David, and came to Mary,
but Joseph entered and rose up that he might be the head.

She took the name of the supposed husband, while not
approaching,
because in the number of the men, the women could not
enter.

Because he was her husband, he was spoken of in the
genealogies;
that she generated in her virginity is testified by the truth.

Because of all these things that I said, it was necessary that he
be the spouse of Mary,
and so the Son of God might dwell in her.

Because Joseph the just one would minister to the way of the
Son,
it was necessary that he be a husband to His Mother in her
virginity.

Secretly he attended to the hidden mystery and no one was
aware,
until our Lord showed the world who was His Father.

661 By His deeds, He taught the world that He is the Son of God;
blessed be the hidden One who appears openly to give life to
Adam.

Concerning the Holy Mother of God, Mary, When She Went to Elizabeth to See the Truth That Was Told to Her by Gabriel

Lord of all, let my harp be stirred by You for Your glory,
for because of You whoever is eager is able to speak to You.

My Lord, generate for me sounds and words, even music,
that my mouth may speak about You profusely.

My tongue will be Your pen, a scribe full of wisdom,
and with it will lovingly show forth Your discourse to be
    heard.

Let Your love stir me to speak to You with discernment
with an unworthy soul full of wonder concerning Your birth.

662 Son of the Most High, who willed to be from mortals,
in You my poor word is raised up to Your Father's high place.

You are greater, my Lord, than reason and speech,
and small are the minds and the intellects to describe You.

The discourse about You is hidden from earthly beings and
    from heavenly ones;
Your tale is hidden from spiritual beings and from bodily
    creatures.

Neither men nor angels are sufficient for You,
because Your miracle is more sublime than earthly beings or
    heavenly ones.

If all the peoples would sing praise to You with their
    "hosannas,"
[yet] the word about You would [still] be too exalted to be
    uttered by them.

A womb enclosed You, yet how can a word be sufficient for
    You?
A womb carried You, yet who does not fear to speak of You?

Arms carried You, but for someone to speak of You is
    audacious;
breasts have nourished You, yet not to marvel [at You] is an
    ingratitude.

Heaven stood in awe, it diminished, it wasted from Your
    greatness,
but a womb received, held, and carried Your glory.

Because of these things, the learned man stumbles when he
    beholds You;
the word of the wise one is defeated since it does not suffice
    for You.

Whenever the mind beheld that heaven is full of Your
    greatness,
it saw Your Shekinah dwelling in the womb; it is troubled.

On this account the disputant stumbles without knowing You;
his word is entangled in strife without praising You.

663 In faith, without stumbling because of Your lowliness,
grant me to receive You in my thoughts with wonder.

The Wonderful One

> Even the sky is small for You, my Lord, if You will it,
> but the womb of Mary is big for You because You so willed.

> Because You so willed, a womb has contained You;
> unless You so willed, all the ages would not suffice You,

> Son of the Lord of the universe.

> Because it pleased You to dwell in the womb, in spite of Your
>   greatness,
> on this account, You are a marvel to the one who knows You.

> Even when the womb of Mary bore You, because it pleased You,
> all the ages were filled with You, because such You are.

> Even if there were no place within the ends [of the earth] that
>   was not filled with You,
> You were dwelling in a span of flesh because You so willed.

> For a great place, indeed, was not sufficient to contain You,
> nor are You straitened by a little place if You stay there.

> Heaven is small but the maiden is great according to Your will,
> for that one is inadequate but this one is fruitful because You
>   strengthened her.

> Mary's conception fills me with wonder,
> and I am not able to speak of her story except with
>   inexplicable wonder.

664 For how must I not marvel at Him who was in Mary;
> He was also in His Father, all in all but not contained.

> He is in the bosom of the Father, the Ancient of Days and
>   ancient of all;
> within a womb the Babe is conceived—He is one and the
>   same.

All of Him sits on the flaming chariot;
all of Him dwells in the womb of flesh—He is one and the same.

All of Him in heaven is hidden and is glorified with His
    Begetter;
all of Him on earth is carried in the Child—He is one and the
    same.

Obscure in essence, concealed in greatness, clothed in flames,
    wearing bright fire—
He is glorious on the throne, awesome between the wheels.

Stirring the cherubim, reverenced by the seraphim, glorified
    within the ranks;
His garment is shining, His clothing glorious, fire surrounds
    Him.

The flame is agitated by the stirring and it fears Him,
but the maiden Mother conceives and carries Him.

Mary, "Second Heaven"

He is great while not diminishing in His small state,
and if He had feared lest He be reduced, He would not be
    great.

If the small womb of Mary had not contained Him,
heaven that is greater would have held Him, and He would
    have been contained.

Because He dwelt in her womb, it is known that He is without
    limit;
heaven and earth are small for Him to dwell in.

If a small place had been too small for Him, and a big one too
    big,
He would not have been great because in a small place He
    would be contained.

665 And because the great heaven and a small womb are worthy of
Him,
by this He makes known His incomprehensible greatness.

There is no place in the bosom of His Father that is not filled
with Him,
but because He dwelt in a womb, He did not overflow from it,
because He was filling it all.

The stretches of heaven are not vast for Him, because He is
bigger than all;
the humble maiden is not small for Him, because He extends
and contracts Himself.

He descended and dwelt in her and her small womb was large
for Him,
for a small place cannot straighten or constrain Him.

Heaven and Mary were for Him equal when He dwelt in her,
yet not equal, for to the one who beholds her Mary is greater.

Heaven is His throne and Mary His Mother, and behold they
are not equal,
for the throne does not resemble the Mother, because the
Mother is greater.

Heaven and Mary, singly He chose the both of them;
He made one of them a throne and the other a Mother.

I will not call heaven "Mary," lest be dishonored the Mother of
the King
by the name of His throne, and He become angry with me.

Now judge truly my words, O wise one,
and if it would not provoke you, explain to us who is greater.

Heaven beholds the maiden Mother and the Only-Begotten;
between the two of them who is greater, and who is more
blessed?

666 Which of them is nearer to Him and dearer to Him,
and more precious to Him and more united to Him?

Heaven did not give milk to Him who became a Babe,
but He seized the breast in the bosom of Mary who had
become His Mother.

Heaven did not conceive Him nor bear Him nor suckle Him,
but she bore, embraced, raised Him, and to her belongs a
blessing.

O Mary, you are blessed among women and full of blessings
without my word laying hold of your mystery that it be
contained by it.

Pure Virgin and Mother, exalted above marriage,
full of blessings for which a myriad of mouths are not
adequate!

Conception is in your womb but virginity in your members;
milk is in your breasts, but your womb is closed to marital
coupling.

The suffering of intercourse of ordinary married women is
removed from you,
but in your womb dwells the Fruit making all mothers glad.

Your body is free from the way of coupling,
yet your womb is filled with a Babe, beloved of nurturers!

A man is far, but birth without marriage is near; on account of
this the learned ones are defeated;
they are not capable of understanding you.

O cloud of mercy,[1] which is full of hope for all the world,
all the earth that had been ravaged was pacified by it.

---

[1] "Cloud of Mercy," 3 Enoch 22c.2.

667 O ship of riches, in which the Father's treasury was sent
to the poor in a needy place and it enriched them!

O field, which without a ploughman yielded a sheaf of life,
and all creation that had been needy was satiated by it.

O virginal vine, which though not pruned gave a cluster,
behold by whose wine creation, which was mourning, rejoices.

Daughter of poor ones, who were mother to the only rich One,
behold whose treasures are lavished on mendicants to enrich
    them.

She was a letter in which the secret of the Father was written,[2]
which by her flesh He revealed to the world that the world
    might be renewed by it.

O letter—it was not a case of it being written and then sealed;
but it was sealed first and only then written—a great wonder!

For while it was sealed, it was mystically written;
although not opened, it was read clearly.

She became a letter, and what was written on her is the Word;
when it was read, the earth was enlightened by its tidings.

He stooped to lowliness because it was easy for Him,
but His greatness rushed after Him that He be honored by it.

The Birth of Our Lord

Because He became a Babe, babes in the womb longed for
    Him;
He became an infant and the star announced that He was God.[3]

Since He was glorious, the heavens were narrating His glory;
since He was great, babes of wedlock brought tidings of Him.

[2]Mary as "letter," see Homily 1, n. 34.
[3]Cf. Mt 2.2.

668 The firmament sent a messenger to distant places,
to announce to the earth[4] that the Lord of the heavens had
risen from the depths.

And babes from the womb offered a precursor
that the world might know that the One who forms babes[5]
was dwelling in the maiden.

A Babe and a star revealed to creation His conception and His
Birth,
lest He be dishonored because of the frailty into which He had
descended.

The heavens sang His glory with their row of lights,
and babes proclaimed His power in the rejoicing of their
parts.

Light and sound were His heralds in their manifestations;[6]
one from heaven and the other from the depths brought
tidings.

In the barren womb of the daughter of Levi, His generation is
awesome,
indeed, the enclosed babe proclaims Him with great wonder.

The Mother of God and Elizabeth

The loving encounter of the kin again amazes me;
word of it moves me to manifest its beauty.

The maiden and the old woman granted me a tale full of
wonder;
love moves me, that while I am marveling, I may speak of it.

[4]Cf. Ps 18.2.
[5]See Homily 2, n. 31.
[6]"Manifestations," *schemata*, 1 Cor 7.31. The term occurs in Philo and Josephus,
see Kittel, *Theological Dictionary*, 7:956.

The Virgin with her love, also the sterile one with her
    gladness,
required me to give a sermon for both of them.

They looked at each other like regions in their manifestations:
East and West, in which their times are depicted.

669 The old woman is similar to this region in which evening is
    depicted,
which enshrouds and buries the light in its old age.

The maiden is similar to the east, the mother of the early
    morning
that carries the day in its bosom to bring it to earth.

Morning and evening look at each other lovingly,
so that in youth and in old age a sense of wonder may
    increase.

Morning that carries the great Sun of Righteousness,
and evening in which is the star that proclaims the Light.

The great King dwells in the maiden and weaves crowns;
the old woman carries the servant announcing the kingdom.

In virginity, the Lord of natures is celebrated;
in sterility, the son of Levites is magnified.

The maiden carries the Ancient Babe, who gave birth to
    Adam;
the old woman [carries] the child who is created today in
    matrimony.

In the woman of Judah is the lion's whelp of whom Jacob
    wrote;[7]
in the Levite, a priest[8] who opened up Baptism.

---

[7]Cf. Gen 49.9.
[8]Lk 3.3.

This Virgin came, great and full of holiness,
to rejoice with the old sterile one at the novel conception.

Each met the other, the one full of blessings and the daughter
  of the Levites,
boats of treasures from which the whole world was enriched.

670 Two who brought forth: the One who was announced and the
      announcer,
with the same message full of salvation for the whole world.

The maiden visited her and spoke a luminous greeting[9] in her
  ears;
immediately the enclosed babe was aware and began leaping
  for joy.[10]

It was beautiful for Mary that she should speak peace,
for she sowed peace for those far and near.

She was as a treasure full of peace for all mankind;
great peace was hidden in her for those who were at enmity.

She offered peace as also she had received peace, from on
  high,
which was for the whole world.

Peace was spoken profusely from her mouth;
it was fitting for the blessed one to proclaim it.

Peace [was] in her womb, and with her lips she gave peace,
and the babe who heard began cheekily making merry.

The Israelites were given to pleasure in dancing for joy before
  God,
when He is carried about in [special] places.

---

[9]"Luminous greeting," *shafya,* see Homily 1, n. 19.
[10]Cf. Lk 1.44.

King David was dancing before the Ark,[11]
and he did not observe the order of royalty because of the
　　great joy of his heart.

John the Baptist in His Mother's Womb

Also John, when he was a babe, danced for joy even better
　　than David;
being a babe, he did not comply with an age that was not his.

671　The Mother, Virgin and blessed, was even more beautiful than
　　the Ark full of mysteries of the house of God.

And he, David, exulted with reverence before the Ark,
for this had prefigured that John would dance before Mary.

That a king might dance was unheard of, except David,
nor a babe who exulted, because the one was prefigured in the
　　other.

Prophets and kings prefigured the way of the Son of God;
when He had come, He fulfilled the figures that were seeking
　　Him.

While the Ark was being carried, David had danced for joy,
so that he, too, might attest to the figure of the King, His Lord.

He typified in figure the way of Mary with John,
for also that maiden was the ark of the Godhead.

The Lord of mysteries had dwelt within her and, because of
　　this,
the babe had danced for joy like that king filled with exploits.

She was carried as an ark full of scriptures;
in her dwelt the interpretation of the mysteries of prophecy.

---

[11]Cf. 2 Kg (2 Sam) 6.14–16.

So that her magnificence might be greater than that of the
    Ark,
the babe exulted for she was adorned in a wonderful way.

The agitation of the silent babe in the closed womb was
    unrestrained;
merry the rejoicing in a womb so long mournful.

And how many of these things were said by John in his
    mother's womb
while he danced for joy because of his Lord!

672 "Behold the Fashioner of all babes, who was made a Babe,
and the great One, of whom heaven is full, dwelt in a womb.

"This is the divine Lamb who came to be[12]
the great victim for sinners, to save them!

"This One takes on Himself the sin of the world
and frees mankind from bondage.

"This One makes His light shine in Sheol amidst the darkness,
and loosens and brings forth Adam, who was bound in the
    house of perdition.[13]

"This One tears up the deed that Eve wrote and owed to her Lord
when He cast her out from amidst the trees.[14]

"This Babe frees the babes of mothers
from that curse of the sentence by His new Birth.

"This One who dwells in a small womb and it carries Him;
heaven is great, but it does not enclose Him, that He be
    contained by it."

[12]Cf. Jn 1.29.

[13]In Syriac literature, the theme of Christ's descent into Sheol is found already
in the second century Odes of Solomon. As depicted in the icon of the Resurrection,
Christ in His descent frees Adam and the righteous of the Old Testament, see 1 Pet 3.19.

[14]Cf. Gen 3.16.

By the Holy Spirit the babe was greatly moved in his mother's
  womb;
he made known who the Son was and announced Him
  beyond nature.

Where there is no possibility for babes to speak,
there he preached what marvelously he had begun to make
  known.

First he announced Him in a place hidden from tidings,
that when preaching Him in the midst of the assemblies, he
  would not be reproached.

673 He made a veil for his preaching in the world,
so that his word might be revealed without risking hypocrisy.

He showed that he knew Him although he had not seen Him,
  so that when he did see Him and say, "This is He,"[15]
no one should be doubtful concerning His manifestation.

Before going forth he announced Him to the world,
so that, as soon as he had gone forth, no one might flee from
  his testimony when he was proclaiming Him.

He overcame nature, and beyond nature he witnessed to the Son,
that it might be revealed that the Lord of natures dwelt in the
  maiden.

All the [things] of the Son are too exalted for interpretation;
they are not heard except with the ear of faith.

All His things were new and were not understood;
they are not perceived except in wonder by the one who
  loves.[16]

---

[15]Cf. Jn 1.29.

[16]"Wonder," in Syriac theology, functions as a principle of interpretation and, as such, as an alternative to scientific inquiry. For a relevant discussion, see Sebastian P. Brock, *The Luminous Eye,* 2nd ed. (Kalamazoo, MI: Cistercian Publications, 1992), 43–46.

For Mary, wonder, and for Elizabeth, great astonishment;
new visions in that one and this one, for those who discern.

For both of them the word is inept and speech ceases;
silence, in wonder, overshadows narration.[17]

To which one, indeed, will the word come to speak,
for, behold, both of them are exalted beyond interpretation.

Drawing near to Mary, speech is silenced,
because it sees tokens of virginity and the Babe who dwells
within them.

And coming upon Elizabeth, discourse is troubled,
for from within her womb it hears a herald with astonishment.

674 The Virgin is with child and, behold, the babe of the sterile
one leaps for joy;
a double measure of astonishment for glorious babes—whom
should we behold?

One is celibate yet without coupling there is fruit in her;
in the womb of the other, before birth, her babe dances for joy.

Whom must we admire: the old woman whose babe has
become a herald,
or the maiden in whom there is a Babe, yet she remained a virgin?

This one did not know contact with men, yet her womb is full,
and that one, her babe prepares the way before being born.

She who is without marital union is full of wonder for her
pure conception,
and the babe of the one who has not given birth stirs with the
proclamation.

[17]On "silence" see Ignatius of Antioch, *To the Ephesians* 15.1–2, 19.1; *To the Mag-nesians* 8.2. For text and commentary, see William R. Schoedel, *Ignatius of Antioch: A Commentary on the Letters of Ignatius of Antioch*, Hermeneia (Philadelphia, PA: Fortress Press, 1985).

Nature and the way of women is powerless in both of them,
because their affairs have not been guided by nature.

That a babe in his mother's womb be aware is not natural,
nor that a woman be with child without marital union.

Therefore, a word full of wonder is required of us,
because only with admiration can we speak of these things
that have taken place.

The greeting of Mary came in by the ear; the vigilant one heard it,
and immediately began to prepare the way as he had been sent.[18]

A voice rushed from Mary's lips announcing to the babe in the womb
that his Lord had come, and it began to dance for joy.[19]

675 The Son of the Virgin apportions the Spirit,
and John, indeed, in the womb is filled with His gift.

He sent the Holy Spirit to the silent babe;
He filled him with power and proclamation there where he was.

A revelation had descended from Him to John;
the course of apostleship began before its time.

By the mouth of Mary, her Son stretched forth the Spirit to
His envoy,[20] from womb to womb;
and he received it while he was in his mother.[21]

With Mary's voice the Holy Spirit was sent out unto the barren one,
and she was filled with great strength.

That One who had breathed the Holy Spirit on the twelve[22]
breathed on the babe,
and it was moved by the Spirit to dance for joy.

[18]Cf. Lk 1.76.
[19]Cf. Lk 1.41–44.
[20]Cf. Lk 1.41–44.
[21]Cf. Lk 1.15.
[22]Jn 20.22.

He lay still in the maiden, giving the Spirit and [the gift of]
   prophecy,[23]
for no one is able to receive anything except through Him.[24]

Elizabeth's Praise

The Holy Spirit filled Elizabeth when He visited John,
and the old lady began speaking in prophecy.

She heard the greeting and received the Spirit and cried out;
before Mary she bowed and lovingly said,

"Blessed are you among women, O maiden, and blessed is the
   beloved Fruit that dwells in holiness in your womb.

"Blessed is your conceiving, and blessed is the Babe of your
   virginity;
blessed is your Babe who removed the curse from the earth.[25]

676   "Who grants me that you come to me,[26] O blessed one?
You bear the great One who has willed to come to lowliness.

"Mother of the King, with how many mouths to praise that
   One who dwells in you, who has come and visited me in
   my poor house!

"A Flame dwells in your blessed womb,[27]
and even the seraphim are shaken if they look at it.

"The living Flame and the Kindler of worlds is silent in you;
that Flame that purifies the thorns of false worship when it is
   uncovered.

---

[23]See again the sense of Elizabeth's prophetic role according to Origen in FOC
94:28–32.

[24]Cf. 1 Cor 12.3.

[25]Gen 3.17–18.

[26]Cf. Lk 1.43.

[27]Cf. Ex 3.2ff. See also Targum Jonathan on Zech 2.9: "And my Memra will be
to her, says the Lord, like a wall of fire encircling her round about, and I will make

"That Flame that kindled the world fills your womb;
the thorns[28] that are planted in all the earth are consumed by it.

"A lion's whelp rises from you,[29] O glorious one;
all the wolves flee from it when they see it.

"You carry the Sun whose rays give light to the universe;[30]
all the darkness that oppresses the world is dissipated by Him.

"A great light is hidden and covered by your virginity,
a light that banishes all shadows from the lands.

"An ocean is enclosed in you, for the earth is too small to contain it;
by it, sin is drowned that had overwhelmed all mankind.

"O Virgin full of wonder, who grants me that you come to me,
because your Son is the Lord and the prime Mover who
    cannot be dishonored.

677 "O maiden in whom the Ancient of Days[31] willed to be carried,
how can I encompass a greeting from your lips?

"O lady full of blessings and graces,
how can I hear your voice and see your beauty and rejoice in
    your Son!

"The rock that brought forth streams[32] cannot be compared
    to you,
because living waters go forth from you to the whole world.

my Shekinah dwell in her midst in honor." Found in Kevin J. Cathcart and Robert P. Gordon, eds, *The Targum of the Minor Prophets*, The Aramaic Bible 14 (Wilmington, DE: Michael Glazier, 1989). On God as fire see: Deut 4.24; Lam 4.11; 3 En 42. See also Exodus Rabbah 20.16, 40.4 in *Midrash Rabbah*, trans. H. Freedman and Maurice Simon and *Pesikta Rabbati,* trans. William G. Braude, 2 vols (New Haven, CT: Yale University Press, 1968), 30:3; 35:2.

[28] Cf. Gen 3.18.
[29] Cf. Gen 49.9.
[30] Cf. Mal 4.2.
[31] Cf. Dan 7.9, 13, 22.
[32] Cf. Ex 17.6; Num 20.11; 1 Cor 10.4.

"Your portion is greater than the glorious chariot of the
    visions,[33]
because that One whom you carry, behold, He grows in you
    yet enriches you."

Mary said, "Speak, old woman, for it is right for you;
speak and cry out about the conception that confounds me greatly.

"Your discourse is similar to that of Archangel Gabriel,
as the discourse of that one was likewise exalted when he
    spoke with me.

"Who revealed to you the mystery that I heard from Gabriel;[34]
since I did not promulgate the Watcher's mystery, who told
    you of it?

"Now did Gabriel tell you how the mystery came to pass?
He indeed is the only mediator in the mystery of which I have
    spoken."

The barren one said, "Gabriel did not reveal the mystery,
but the babe who is in me is the sharer of that secret that you
    have borne.

"He shows to me that his Lord dwells in you, O blessed one;
from him I have learned who He is and whose Son, and how
    He is.

678 "Since I saw you, he has not ceased urging me[35]
to bless you, to do reverence, to rejoice with his Lord who has
    come to him.

"As soon as the greeting came to my ears from your lips,
the babe whom I carry leaped in me with great joy.

---

[33]Cf. Ezek 1.
[34]Cf. Lk 1.28ff.
[35]Cf. Lk 1.44.

"He shook in me and I trembled, and he danced in me and I
    marveled at you;
behold, the King, his Lord, quickens me to worship.

"He is solicitous and gay, merry and quick, and full of love;
he behaves impudently because of his Lord who has come to
    him."

Praise of the Mother of God

The maiden said, "I magnify the Lord who has done a great
    miracle for me;
by His grace He has filled me with wonder.[36]

"For henceforth all nations of the whole world at all times
will speak great things of me.

"In the world I will be a great parable full of wonder;
all mouths will speak of me, profusely.

"The sea and the earth and all the world will give thanks
    because of me,
since my mouth is too small to give praise for these things.

"My name will be brought to distant lands;
all frontiers will speak of me while marveling.

"The entire order of mother[hood] will be made glad in me,
since the Fruit that I have borne restrains death from their
    offspring.

"From this time forward womankind will be blessed in me,
for through me the reproach of Eve is removed from
    womanhood.[37]

[36]Lk 1.46–56.
[37]Cf. Gen 3.16.

679   "The Babe who is in me will crush the head of the great
      serpent;[38]
  by Him, Adam, having been expelled, is restored to his
      heritage.

"Now therefore Eve, who had been ashamed, may show her
      face,
and lift her head because of the Lord of Paradise who dwelt in
      me.

"The babes will dance for joy and soon after all the dead,
because of the Lord of all the peoples who has visited them in
      their abodes.[39]

"Let a crown of glory be offered to Him by pregnant women,
for He has dwelt in a womb, so that their beloved might be
      blessed by Him.

"Also let the poor glorify the name of the Son of the rich One
who willed to mingle[40] with the poor and enrich them.

"Let all the multitude of virgins praise Him with wonder,
because the great Savior shines forth from them to the whole
      world.

"Let the voice of the young women be lifted up in praise,
because by one of them, behold, hope is brought to the world.

"Let heaven send a great crown to the world, to the earth—his
      sister,
because behold the Lord of heaven is carried by earthly
      creatures."

[38]Cf. Gen 3.15.

[39]Here Christ's presence in Mary's womb is linked with His descent into Sheol. Together with His Baptism in the Jordan, they form the three "wombs" or "abodes" where all time and space are transfigured.

[40]"Mingle," *hlat* and *mazzeg* are variously used by Syriac writers such as Ephrem, Aksenaya (Philoxenus of Mabbug) and Jacob to describe the union between Christ and the Church; the two natures of Christ; the union of the soul with the Holy Spirit.

How delightful were those words that were spoken in the
    house of the priest,
because of the conception of the blessed one.

How stupendous were those wombs carrying babes,
full of wonder by which the whole world was adorned.

680 The mystery of the Father has been told amidst the pure,
while He is lovingly praised between the two of them.

Then the house of the high priest became a sanctuary;
Majesty was humbly served in it.

All sorts of novelties that are usually not done were there:
a babe dances for joy, a virgin conceives, and great is the wonder!

The barren one was made merry by the stirring of the babe
    who caused her to marvel;
the Virgin was rejoicing at the glorious conception that was
    dwelling in her.

It was an abode in which were dwelling all riches, explanation
    of mysteries,
and interpretation of the books of the prophets.

The Word and the Voice

The Word and the Voice[41] were there in the two wombs:
in Elizabeth there was the Voice and in Mary, the Word.

The Word and the Voice are without marital union and with
    marital union;
the Voice dwells with coupling and the Word without it.

So thus the Voice and the Word are in their manifestations;[42]
because also nature thus seeks to praise them.

[41]Cf. Lk 3.4; Jn 1.4.
[42]"Manifestation," Phil 2.7. See n. 6.

Without marital union the Word dwells within the mind;
without coupling it is perfect and still where it is.

But when thought considers revealing its place,
it sends the voice to prepare the way for hearing.

681 Indeed, the voice is impelled to go out by union
with the mouth and the teeth, and with the tongue that sends
     it forth.

Suffering conceives and gives birth to it from its lips,
by the partnership that the teeth effect with the tongue.

These corporeal instruments, which were alien when they
     were united,
have generated the voice that by it the word might be
     transmitted to its place.

By the union that happens to the lips with their quivering,
they generate the voice of the word, bringing it forth to
     manifestation.

Likewise, John, whose conception was by union,
he (who) is the Voice that had been sent in front of the Word.

Through union he was conceived because without union there
     is no voice;
he was prepared for preaching by union.

He was formed in the proximity of separate bodies;
as in corporeal vessels, the voice hastens to the hearing.

It is not possible that there be the voice without coupling;
no one comes to birth without marital union.

Even John who is called Voice was a man;
(with)in marital union his mother conceived him in the
     embrace of his father.

And lest his conception in the womb be without wonder,
an old barren woman conceived him after a long time, adding
to the wonder.

He was held in honor as much as nature would permit,
that his story might shine in the world, being a child of
barrenness.

682 The Virgin was chosen for the Word by the divine Majesty,
for the Word has no need at all of coupling.

A pure maiden, who was not joined in marriage, was chosen
for the Word,
because her conceiving and her giving birth were remote from
marital union.

Marriage occurred for the Voice, which never is produced
without marital union;
a Virgin for the Word, because He is entirely without need of
coupling.

This is the mode of the Word where it is:
it is concealed in the soul and does not draw near to
partnership.

It is hidden in the mind and without coupling dwells in the
soul;
there is no way for marital union to happen to it.

Because of this, the Word chose for Himself a Virgin who is
exalted beyond marital union,
that from her He might appear bodily.

He sent that Voice that was conceived in marital union,
that he might prepare the way and straighten a path until He
come.

Also the Voice precedes the Word to the hearing;
it knocks at it to open the door for the Word to enter.

The message of the Word brings the Voice to the door of the
ear,
so that the Voice hastens before Him, and by him the Word
becomes manifest to the hearing.

The Voice divides the air and makes plain a way for the Word,
that He might travel; when the Voice reached the door of
the ear, he remained behind; that One entered.

John hastened from within the womb to the river,
as a voice from the mouth to the ear, but he never comes
nearer.

683   He did not enter the chamber of the Bridegroom so as to
marry;
he betrothed the bride of his Lord, then being loyal, went away.[43]

In the sanctuary there is one who enters into the Majesty;
the ordinary priest does not pass within the veil.[44]

The voice remains outside of the ear, but the word goes in;
indeed, how far the voice's region extends is known.

It does not go out from the mind with the word when it is sent,
nor does it enter the hearing with it when the word is
manifest.

It is the word's minister between the mouth and hearing,
but it does not reach to where the word comes and to where it
goes.

So with John, who became the Voice to the Word, his Lord,
the limit is known where he began and where he made an end.

He began his preaching from within the womb;
its completion was at the baptismal fount.

---

[43]Christ is the "Bridegroom," See Homily 5, n. 25.
[44]Heb 9.7; Lev 16.

He received with rejoicing the imprint of the Bridegroom
    from within his mother;
he went and laid it down by the ears of the bride at the
    ablution.

As Voice, he hastened and brought perception of the Word
    then desisted;
he announced Him to the crowd, and as soon as they
    recognized Him, he withdrew from Him.

Then the Bridegroom entered and attended to His mystery
    that had been announced,
and John desisted, like a voice when it is sent forth.

Because he was the Voice, as Isaiah had prophesied of him,
therefore, he had exulted before the Word with great rejoicing.

684 The Word in the glorious womb of the Virgin made a sign;
and the Voice was moved to appear openly out of
    barrenness.

The Son of the Virgin secretly made a sign from within the
    womb;
the son of marriage danced openly for joy while he was in his
    mother.

The gesture of the Word stirs up the Voice to the hearing,
and the Word impels the Voice to go out and proclaim the
    Word to those outside.[45]

The Voice is the messenger of the Word, and His evangelist;
he makes Him known, also showing Him forth and extolling
    Him.

Thus the Voice is prefigured in prophecy;[46]
he is the herald that was sent before the Word.

[45]Mk 4. 11.
[46]Cf. Is 40.3.

When he was questioned by the Hebrews as to who he was, he
    made known that he was the Voice[47]
who was sent in order to preach concerning the Word.

He did not call himself either prophet or Elijah,[48]
but a voice corresponding to the deed for which he was
    destined.

He gave heed to his work for which the Word had sent him as
    Voice;
from this deed he gave himself a name when they asked him:

"I am the Voice," so that from his name all men might know
that, after the Voice, the Word hurries to the hearers.

He also had said that "after me He comes and I am the
    Voice";[49]
namely, to show with this, that it is the Word whom he
    announces.

685   In this way, he bestirred him in the womb of his mother,[50]
while the Word moved him, that he might make merry
    bringing

Great wonder in the Word and the Voice for those who are
    discerning;
blessed is the Word concerning whose manifestation the Voice
    proclaimed.

[47]Cf. Jn 1.23.
[48]Cf. Jn 1.21.
[49]Cf. Jn 1.27; 1.30.
[50]Lk 1.41, 44.

Concerning the Burial—That Is to Say, the Death of the Holy Virgin Mother of God, Mary—and How She Was Buried by the Apostles

Son, who in Your love inclined heaven and descended to
  earth;
and put on a body and became man from the daughter of
  David!

Mystical Offspring from whom the heights and the depths are
  filled,
fill me with Your mystical instruction that brought about two
  worlds.

Only-Begotten Son, who fashioned man from nothing,
restore the discourse in my weary mind that I may sing to
  You.

Son, who firmly fixed ten mortal senses in the mortal body,
stay my thoughts and bring them to the place of Your Father.

Christ, who have given the Spirit of life to man whom You
  created,
pour into me Your living discernment, filled with wonder.

710 Hidden One, who are concealed even from the Watchers, and
  they do not see You, shine upon me in stillness so that I
  may proclaim openly about Your Mother.

O You, who healed the unclean man who had been brought
    near to You,
restore and heal the body and the soul of those who await You.

Light of Christ, which illumines the eyes that are darkened,
let Your light shine forth on my frailty, and I will be
    enlightened by You.

Lord of mankind, who wanted to become human in the flesh,
and rested upon and dwelt within the pure mother, the
    daughter of lights.

O You, who dwelt with her for nine months and came to birth,
may my mind produce gifts of praise at Your mystical Nativity.

O You, who were cherished with lullabies by the pure Mother,
may my tongue pour forth all praise of Your sweetness.

Son, who have visited us and fulfilled the whole Economy,
grant me to speak of the burial of the faithful one.

Your Mother endured many sufferings for Your sake;
every grief encompassed her at Your crucifixion.

How much sighing and sorrowful tears did her eyes shed
when they enshrouded You and brought You to rest within the
    tomb.

How much terror the Mother of mercy felt at Your burial
when the guards at the sepulcher seized her lest she draw near
    to You.

711 She endured sufferings when she saw that You were hanged on
        the cross,
that with a spear they had pierced Your side on Golgotha,

and when the Jews had sealed the sepulcher
in which had been placed Your living body that gives life and
    remits debts.

The Way of All Generations

> And to this Mother, who endured these things for You,
> the end had come to depart to the world that is full of
>   blessings.

> The time came to proceed on the way of all the generations
> who have gone and come to the end with great quaking.

> Prior to all the generations, Adam journeyed on that way,
> and good Seth and the generations of his just sons of former
>   times.[1]

> The pure and innocent generation of righteous Noah traveled
>   on it,
> and that of Shem and of Japheth and of Ham, the sons who
>   were on the earth.

> Abraham and Isaac, the good workers, followed them,
> and also the righteous who were on the earth from generation
>   to generation.

> Jacob, the just and humble one, went in that way,
> and after him the twelve patriarchs, his beautiful sons.

> Joseph traveled there and the sons of Ephraim and Judah,
> and with them that humble Moses and the glorious Hur.

> After him came Joshua, son of Nun, an admirable man,
> and Aaron the priest and all the tribes of Levi.

712 David the king and the generation of his kingdom, also Daniel
>   of Babylonia, a man most pleasing,[2]
> and with him the three innocent children in the furnace.[3]

---

[1]Gen 5.6–8.
[2]Cf. Dan 9.23, Peshitta.
[3]Cf. Dan 3.19ff.; "innocent," *shafya,* see Homily 1, n. 20.

Jephtha, the just, and Gideon, the great, who divided a people,
and Samson, the chosen one, who lost his life because of a
    woman.

The twelve prophets who departed and went with those of
    former times;
also their generations with their times were consumed by death.

Samuel, the pure one, with Jeremiah of great renown;
also Ezekiel, wondrous in prophetic visions.

Isaiah, that faithful admonisher, departed;
all the prophetic company came to an end.

Those of former times departed, and the time of the wicked
    sons came;
the Lord descended to redeem them from error.

The Life and Death of Our Lord

He rested upon[4] and dwelt in her pure womb, full of grace,
this Virgin who, behold, her story is being told by us.

He dwelt in her and settled for nine months unimpeded,
and proceeding in order, the time came for the Birth.

He willed and was born, and in the Jordan received Baptism;[5]
He performed miracles, healed the sick, and purified lepers.

He endured the temptations of the accuser,[6] trampled him,
    conquered him;
the children lauded Him, even the infants with their palm
    branches.[7]

[4]"Rest upon," *aggen,* see Homily 1, n. 14.
[5]Cf. Mt 3.13–17; Mk 1.9ff.; (Lk 3.21; Jn 1.29ff.).
[6]Mt 4.1–15; Mk 1.12ff.; Lk 4.1ff.; "accuser," Rev 12.10.
[7]In the Vespers of Palm Sunday, the Orthodox Church also commemorates
the children, who perceived the theophany of Christ's entry into Jerusalem, as
theologians.

He chose for Himself a company of twelve,[8] full of light,
and Judas, the crafty evil spirit, sprang up from there.

713 He betrayed his master and destroyed his soul and became a
  reproach;
he had fallen from that position of apostleship because he had
  consented.

Then our Lord drew near to death, as we have said;
He died and delivered us, and He rose from the sepulcher and
  took us up with Him.

The Death and Burial of the Mother of God

Unto the Mother of this Jesus Christ, Son of God,
death came that she might taste his cup.

The Lord commanded the exalted hosts above
and the flaming legions, the seraphim of light.

Choirs of Watchers descended in their raiment;[9]
with a loud voice they sang their psalms.

All the righteous of every generation came and gathered
  together,
behold also the righteous and the patriarchs from of old!

The sound of that choir of prophets sings praise,
this one to that one, as seers of truth.

The priests of old and all the company of the sons of Levi,
with their sacrifices and their oblations and their offerings.

That company of the twelve chosen apostles
stands and prepares the virginal body of the blessed one for
  burial.

[8]Cf. Lk 6.12–16; Mt 10.1ff.; Mk 3.13–14.
[9]"Raiment," *schemata,* see Homily 3, n. 6.

John, as a steward of truth,
drew near and enshrouded the glorious body of the blessed
    one.

714 Two illustrious apostles, chosen of the testaments,
were entrusted with that treasure of truth.

The righteous Nicodemus prepared the body of her Son for
    burial[10]
and the body of this Virgin, that chosen son of thunder.[11]

The pastors and their flocks came to the top of the mountain,
reverend priests and ministers with their thuribles.

The winds struck the great dome of the heavens in gusts;
the heights and the depths chanted praise with their harps.

A light shone forth on that place where men and Watchers
were waiting to prepare the most fair one for burial.

As the Lord had descended and prepared His servant Moses
    for burial,[12]
so together with them He buried the Mother, according to the
    flesh.

On a mountain top within luminous clouds,
Moses, the prophet, was buried by God.[13]

And even Mary herself, on that mountain of Galilee,
was buried by the Watchers and also by the angels, together
    with God.

[10]Cf. Jn 19.39.
[11]Cf. Mk 3.17.
[12]Cf. Deut 32.48–52.
[13]Cf. Deut 34.6. See Rashi on the death of Moses and his burial by God. Found in *The Pentateuch with Targum Onkelos, Haphtaroth and Rashi's Commentary,* 5 vols, trans. M. Rosenbaum and Abraham Maurice Silbermann (London: Shapiro, Valentine & Co., 1929–1934).

John, the youthful virgin, drew near and embraced the pure
   mother
who had been committed to him by our Savior.

He was a mediator between God and men
while the Watchers descended with great ineffable solemnity.

715 In a cave of stone, in the new sepulcher of Nicodemus,[14]
they introduced and placed the Son of this blessed one.

And again, this pure Mother of the Son of God
they introduced and placed her in a cave, in a sepulcher from
   a cave of stone.

All that company of the apostles gathered together and stood
   by,
while in truth, their Master (together) with them laid her in
   the grave.

Ranks and companies, also choirs of the sons of light;
a clamor of Watchers and a multitude of burning flames.[15]

Fiery seraphim with wings closely covered by flames,
with legions and their heavenly divisions.

Mighty cherubim who are yoked beneath His throne[16]
are moved by wonder to give praise with their hosannas.

Followers of Gabriel, a glowing fiery multitude,
are variously transformed in their natures.

---

[14]Cf. Mt 27.60.

[15]Ps 104.4; Heb 1.7; 2 En 1.4f, 9.1–2, 29.3(?); 3 En 7, 15, 22. See also Braude, *Pesikta Rabbati* 33:10: "The Fire of the Divine Word is more fierce than the fire of the angels, for the angels come merely from the fire under the throne of glory, the fiery river which Daniel saw. 'A fiery stream issued and came forth from before Him' (Dan 7.10), and of this fire they are created; but the fire of the Divine Word comes directly from the right hand of the Holy One, blessed be He."

It is a common idea in rabbinic literature that angels are formed out of fiery matter.

[16]Cf. Ezek 1.4ff. See the discussion of Merkabah imagery: Homily 2, n. 31.

Followers of Michael, full of movement in their descent,
feasting, rejoicing, making merry this day with their alleluias.

Heaven and the air of glory[17] were filled with celestials
who journeyed and came down to the place of earth.

A sweet and pure fragrance blew from the thuribles
of the exalted multitude when they met to descend to earth.

The demons fled and the hosts of darkness;
also all the souls that were afflicted were again assuaged.

716 The demons fled the souls in which they were;
there was rest for those who were being tempted by their cruelty.

The evil demons were disturbed and agitated,
for they saw the sign that only happened because of our Lord.

They saw heaven discharging multitudes of hosts;
the air was utterly sanctified with sweet fragrance.[18]

New sounds were heard from all the birds,
which were chanting in ranks according to their natures.

All living creatures made a joyful sound of praise in their places;
all the earth was stirred by their shouts of joy.

The heavens and the mountains and all the plains that were
    adorned
broke forth in praise when the virginal body was being laid in
    the grave.

[17]"Air of glory," see *Sefer Yetsira*, ch. 1:10–14; ch. 3:2–8, in David R. Blumenthal, *Understanding Jewish Mysticism* (New York: KTAV Publishing House, 1978). For the discussion of "air of glory" in St Ephrem see, Nicolas Séd, "Les hymnes sur le Paradis de s. Ephrem et les traditions juives," *Le Muséon* 81 (1968): 494–99.

[18]"Sweet fragrance," Song 4.16; 3 En 23.18. See also *Numbers Rabbah* 13.2 (trans. Freedman and Simon): "In the hereafter the Holy One, blessed be He, will prepare a feast for the righteous in the Garden of Eden, and there will be no need either of balsam or of choice spices, for the north wind and the south wind will sweep through and sprinkle about all the perfumes of the Garden of Eden, and they will exhale their fragrance."

All living creatures made a joyful sound of praise in their
> places;
all the earth was stirred by their shouts of joy.

All trees, with their fruits and produce,
were sprinkled with dew, the sweet fragrance of their gladness.

All the flowers, which were beautiful in their variety,
sent forth perfume like sweet spices sending forth fragrance.

The waters and the fish and all creeping things within the sea
were aware of this day and were moved to praise.

All creatures, silent or eloquent according to their natures,
rendered the praise that was due.

The Glorification of the Mother of God

717 On this day Adam rejoices and Eve his wife,
because their daughter rests in the place where they are gathered.

On this day the righteous Noah and Abraham rejoice
that their daughter has visited them in their dwelling-place.

On this day Jacob, the honorable old man,
rejoices that the daughter who sprouted from his root has
> called him to life.

On this day the twelve just sons of the lame [one][19]
rejoice greatly and are glad in that she visited them.

On this day let also Judah rejoice greatly,
for behold the daughter who has given life went forth from his
> loins.

On this day let Joseph rejoice, and the great Moses,
for one young maiden has called all mankind to life.

[19]Cf. Gen 32.31.

On this day let Aaron rejoice and Eliezer
and all the tribe of the sons of Levi with their priesthood.

On this day let David, the renowned forefather, rejoice,
because the daughter who was from him has placed a glorious
    crown on his head.

On this day let Samuel rejoice with Jeremiah,
because the daughter of Judah dropped dew on their bones.[20]

Come Ezekiel, trained in prophetic revelation,
if the thing that has occurred is described in your prophecy!

On this day let also Isaiah the prophet rejoice,
because she whom he prophesied, behold, she visits him in the
    place of the dead.

718 On this day all the prophets lifted their heads from their graves,
because they saw the light that shone forth on them.

They saw that death is disquieted and flees from within them;
and [that] the gates of heaven are opened again, and the
    depths of the earth.

The prophets, the apostles, the martyrs, and the priests who
    were gathered together,
also the teachers and the patriarchs and the righteous ones of
    old!

In heaven, the Watchers; in the depths, man; in the air, glory:
when the Virgin Mary was buried as one deceased.

---

[20]"Dew" in rabbinic tradition is an agent of the resurrection. See *Pirke de Rabbi
Eliezer: (The Chapers of Rabbi Eliezer the Great) according to the Text of the Manu-
script belonging to Abraham Epstein of Vienna*, trans. Gerald Friedlander (New York:
Sepher-Hermon Press, 1981 [1st ed. 1916]), 260. See also *Midrash on Psalms*, 2 vols,
trans. William G. Braude, Yale Judaica Series 13 (New Haven, CT: Yale University
Press, 1959), 540: "*The earth trembled,* (Ps 68.9) and at once all the living in the land
of Israel died: But the dead came to life as the Holy One, blessed be He, dropped the
dew of resurrection on them . . ."

A light shone on that company of disciples,
also on her neighbors and her relations and her kindred.

The heavenly company performed their "Holy, Holy, Holy"[21]
unto the glorious soul of this Mother of the Son of God.

Fiery seraphim surrounded the soul of the departed
and raised the loud sound of their joyful shouts.

They shouted and said, "Lift up, O gates, all your heads,[22]
because the Mother of the King seeks to enter the bridal
    chamber of light."[23]

Heaven was full of the sweet music of the angels,
but the depths were troubled, together with the disciples who
    were filled with grief.

The Church on high and that below cried out with one hymn,
for neither those above nor those below could suffice to tell of
    her.

The ranks of that exalted assembly cried out from this one to
    that one,

719 The air dropped living rain on the bones of the sons of the
    Church,
daughter of the Arameans,[24] who did not deny her.

She wove a beautiful crown and set it on her sublime head
on which valuable pearls were laid.

The name of Christ the King, who was crucified on Golgotha,
grants life and sheds forth mercy on the one who invokes Him.

---

[21]Is 6.3; 3 En 35–40. On the celestial *Qedussah*, see P. Alexander's translation and comments in Charlesworth, *Pseudepigrapha* 1:288–92.

[22]Cf. Ps 24.7–9.

[23]"Bridal chamber," *Gnona*, see Brock, *The Luminous Eye*, 115–30. See also Klijn, *Acts of Thomas*, 68 and notes on 172–173.

[24]Arameans/Gentiles.

And also on me a sinner, who am not capable of praising her,
the Mother of mercy who brought You forth in the flesh.

O Son of God, by her prayers make Your peace to dwell
in heaven, in the depths, and among all the counsels of her
    sons.

Make wars to cease, and remove trials and plagues;
bestow calm and tranquility on seafarers.

Heal the infirm, cure the sick, fill the hungry;
be a Father to orphans whom death has left destitute.

In Your pity, drive out devils who harass mankind
and exalt Your Church to the four quarters of the globe, that it
    may sing Your praise.

Watch over priests and purify ministers;
be a guardian of old age and youth.

O Bridegroom Christ,[25] to You be praise from every mouth,
and on us be mercy at all times. Amen, Amen.

End of the Discourse of Mar Jacob Concerning the Death of the Holy Mother of God.

[25]"Bridegroom," the image of the Messiah as Bridegroom, does not occur in the OT according to Jeremias. See Kittel, *Theological Dictionary,* 4:1099–1106. In Syriac theology, the image of Christ the Bridegroom is an important one. See Brock, *The Luminous Eye,* 92–106. Ample quotations from St Ephrem are included.

Additional Bibliography

Alwan, Khalil M. L. "Bibliographie Générale raisonnée de Jacques de Saroug." *Parole de l'Orient* 13 (1986): 313–83.

_____. "L'homme, 'le microcosme' chez Jacques de Saroug." *Parole de l'Orient* 13 (1986): 51–77.

Bou Mansour, Tanios. *La Théologie de Jacques de Saroug*. Kaslik, Liban: Université Saint-Esprit, 1993.

Brock, Sebastian P. "Baptismal themes in the writings of Jacob of Serugh." *Orientalia Christiana Analecta* 205 (1978): 325–47.

Graffin, S.J., François. "The Theme of the Church as Bride in the Syriac Liturgies and Patristic Literature." *Liturgy Bulletin of the Cistercians of the Strict Observance* 24.2 (1990): 77–101.

Hansbury, Mary. "Nature as Soteric: Syriac and Buddhist Traditions." *Aram Periodical: A Festschrift for Dr. Sebastian P. Brock* 5 (1993): 197–217.

Harvey, Susan Ashbrook. "Jacob of Serugh's Homily on Simeon the Stylite." *Ascetical Behavior in Greco-Roman Antiquity: A Sourcebook*. Edited by Vincent L. Wimbush. Minneapolis, MN: Fortress Press, 1990. Pages 15–27.

Jacob of Serug. "On the Establishment of Creation." Translated by Robin Anne Darling. *Biblical Interpretation*. Edited by Joseph Wilson Trigg. Wilmington, DE: Michael Glazier, 1988. Pages 184–202.

Mimouni, Simon Claude. "La tradition littéraire syriaque de l'histoire de la dormition et de l'assomption de Marie." *Parole de l'Orient* 15 (1988–89): 143–168.

Petersen, William L. "The Dependence of Romanos the Melodist upon the Syriac Ephrem: Its Importance for the Origin of the *Kontakion*." *Vigiliae Christianae* 39 (1985): 171–187.

Sony, Behnam M. Boulos. "L'anthropologie de Jacques de Saroug." *Parole de l'Orient* 12 (1979–80): 153–85.

_____. "La Méthode exégétique de Jacques de Saroug." *Parole de l'Orient* 9 (1979–80): 67–103.

Thekeparampil, Jacob. "Jacob of Sarug's Homily on Melkizedeq." *The Harp* 6 (1993): 53–64.

Van Roey, Albert. "La sainteté de Marie d'après Jacques de Saroug." *Ephemerides theologicae lovanienses* 31 (1955): 46–62.

POPULAR PATRISTICS SERIES

ST VLADIMIR'S SEMINARY PRESS
1-800-204-2665 • www.svspress.com

We hope this book has been enjoyable and edifying for your spiritual journey toward our Lord and Savior Jesus Christ.

One hundred percent of the net proceeds of all SVS Press sales directly support the mission of St Vladimir's Orthodox Theological Seminary to train priests, lay leaders, and scholars to be active apologists of the Orthodox Christian Faith. However, the proceeds only partially cover the operational costs of St Vladimir's Seminary. To meet our annual budget, we rely on the generosity of donors who are passionate about providing theological education and spiritual formation to the next generation of ordained and lay servant leaders in the Orthodox Church.

Donations are tax-deductible and can be made at
www.svots.edu/give.
We greatly appreciate your generosity.

To engage more with St Vladimir's Orthodox
Theological Seminary, please visit:

www.svots.edu
online.svots.edu
www.svspress.com
www.instituteofsacredarts.com